CLOSET ESSENTIALS

First published in the United States of America in
2017 by Chronicle Books LLC.

Library of Congress Cataloging-in-Publication
Data available.

ISBN: 9781452166674

Manufactured in China.

Produced by RotoVision, an imprint of
The Quarto Group

Publisher: Mark Searle

Editorial Director: Isheeta Mustafi

Commissioning Editor: Emily Angus

Editor: Katie Crous

Junior Editor: Abbie Sharman

Art Director: Michelle Rowlandson

Book layout: Agata Rybicka and Richard Peters

Illustrations: Clare Shepherd

Photography: Odi Caspi

10 9 8 7 6 5 4 3 2 1

Chronicle Books LLC
680 Second Street
San Francisco, CA 94107
www.chroniclebooks.com

CLOSET ESSENTIALS

60 CORE PIECES AND HOW TO WEAR THEM
ANY TIME · ANY PLACE · ANY WHERE

AMBER MCNAUGHT

CHRONICLE BOOKS

SAN FRANCISCO

CONTENTS

VISUAL INDEX

40

42

44

46

48

50

52

54

56

58

60

62

64

68

70

72

74

76

78

80

82

86

88

90

92

94

96

98

100

102

104

106

108

110

112

116

118

120

122

124

126

128

130

134

136

138

140

142

144

146

148

160

150

156

162

152

158

164

154

166

INTRODUCTION

Fashion stylist Rachel Zoe once said that style is a way to say who you are, without having to speak.

While it's true that many people use clothing successfully to express themselves, the language of style can be a tricky one to learn, and can often leave us feeling like tourists in a foreign land. We know what all the words mean, but putting them together in a way that says exactly what we intended can be harder than we thought, especially when we see the natives swanning around and making it all look so effortless.

Part of the problem, of course, is that we're spoiled for choice. Gone are the days of dress codes and universal trends, when everyone knew exactly what to wear, as well as when and how to wear it. Dress codes are confusing at best (what is "smart/casual," anyway?), and there are so many different styles to choose from that it can be hard to know which one says who you are without the message getting lost in translation.

So, how do you find your way to the style that best expresses your personality, and that also works for your lifestyle and body shape, in the face of so much choice? Well, for some people, style is instinctive: they're those effortless-looking natives who seem to have been born fluent. For the rest of us, there's the capsule wardrobe: a collection of all-time classics that provide the jumping-off point for your own personal style journey. If you're feeling confused by fashion, or are just tired of having a bulging closet yet seemingly have nothing to wear, this book will help you to create and style a classic capsule, which will work for almost any occasion. Then you too can express your personality—without having to say a word.

HOW TO USE THIS BOOK

In this book, you'll find everything you need to create a wardrobe of classic basics, which will transition easily from season to season, and mean you never have to utter/cry the words, "I have absolutely nothing to wear!" ever again. You'll also find suggestions on how to style each piece in different ways, plus background information on the history of each item. (Do you know why ballet flats became fashionable, after years of high heels? You will soon …)

However, before starting to read this book, you need to understand two important things. Firstly, there's no such thing as a universal wardrobe essential. There's no "one size fits all," every one of us is different. With that in mind, it's important to understand that this book is not suggesting that you rush out and buy every single item on the list, or even that you'll want to. Instead of giving you a rigid set of rules, this book sets out to help you build a capsule wardrobe from sixty possible pieces. Secondly, there's no such thing as "bad taste." There are just different kinds of taste, and different ways to wear an item of clothing. That's why each item in this book comes with a set of five styling suggestions, to show you the different ways it can be worn.

The great thing about the classic capsule wardrobe is that it can be adapted to suit a wide range of tastes and styles, and once you have the wardrobe basics, you're free to add in a selection of on-trend pieces whenever you feel like it. The aim of the classic wardrobe isn't to stop you expressing yourself, or lock you into a restrictive style that you can never stray from, but to give you the necessary building blocks from which you can develop your own, unique style. It may or may not be eternal—these days, few of us like or wear the same kind of things for our entire lives—but it will, at least, be yours.

SECTION 1: KNOW YOUR WARDROBE, PAGES 16–37

Before you start to gather your capsule wardrobe, there are some realities you need to face, such as:

• Your budget: Having a realistic idea of your budget will help you to make the right decisions when facing such an array of price tags, quality and materials, and stores and brands from which to buy your capsule wardrobe. Turn to "Shopping on a Budget" (pages 22–27) for more advice.

• Practicality: What do you need your clothes to do for you? Before you start shopping, think about your lifestyle. Learning to shop for the life you actually have, rather than some fantasy life of endless cocktail parties, will make sure you make the most of your wardrobe.

• Climate: Similarly, if you live in a cold climate, there's not much point in filling your closet with summer dresses, no matter how much you love them. Sound familiar? "Dressing for the Seasons" (pages 28–29) should help out here.

• Style: It's also important at this stage to know your body type, and what kind of clothing suits you—refer to the "Style Dos and Don'ts" on pages 32–35 for more.

Looking after your clothes is also important, whether you're going on vacation (see "Vacation Packing," pages 30–31) or simply staying put (see "Clothing Care," pages 36–37) for tips and tricks.

SECTIONS 2–6: CAPSULE ITEMS, PAGES 38–167

Although there's no such thing as "one style fits all," there are certain clothing items that have managed to stand the test of time, and become true classics—the kind of pieces that don't date, that can be worn in multiple different ways, and suit (almost) everyone. These are the items you'll find in this book: there are 60 of them altogether, covering everything from outerwear and accessories to dresses, pants, and tops, and when you put them all together, you'll have the basis of a capsule wardrobe that should see you through just about any situation.

Knowing what to buy is one thing, but having the perfect closet isn't going to make you stylish—if only it were that simple! No, you also have to know how to wear all of those items, and how to combine them into outfits that will work for different occasions: from work to play, and everything in between. As you read through this book, you'll find not only a description of each item, along with some of its history and context, but also five different outfit suggestions for each in the "How to Wear It" section. This section will help you address common dressing dilemmas, and provides a range of beautifully illustrated styling options to help you make the most of your closet, maximizing the use of each item.

Again, not all of the 60 items will work for every body type or style: the little black dress (page 56), for example, or a great pair of skinny jeans (page 120) can work for most people, as long as you make sure you get the right fit and style and, most importantly, have fun experimenting with things you might not otherwise have considered!

KNOW
YOUR
WARDROBE

CAPSULE WARDROBES

If you've ever found yourself stressing over what to wear to a particular event, a capsule wardrobe can clear your mind, free up some time, and generally liberate yourself from the tyranny of the messy closet.

A capsule wardrobe should be comprised of items that are timeless and classic—clothing that will last for years, and which can be worn over and over again. A maximum of sixty items will allow you to create a capsule that will work all year round. It's the antithesis of the fast-fashion movement and, in some ways, a reaction to it, advocating thoughtful spending and investment shopping over rampant consumerism.

WHY CREATE A CAPSULE WARDROBE?

Just in case you were having doubts, here is the main argument of the case for a capsule wardrobe:

You'll always have something appropriate to wear

The irony of the words, "I have nothing to wear!" is that they are most often cried while staring into the yawning abyss of an apparently endless closet. Most of us have so much choice that it becomes overwhelming. The capsule wardrobe will give you fewer clothes, but much more to wear.

It saves you time

By limiting the amount that you own, the capsule wardrobe also limits the number of decisions that you have to make every day, leaving you with more time for the rest of your life.

It provides a shortcut to personal style

Most of the people that we consider to be style icons tend to have a defined sense of style—one that is instantly identifiable as theirs. The limited nature of a capsule wardrobe forces you to think carefully about each item, and to make sure that it's something you will want to wear over and over again.

It saves you money

Buying sixty items at once might not sound thrifty, but many of the items will be things that you already own, but, if not, you don't have to buy the rest in one go (or even at all, if they're not your style). Once you have your capsule, it should last for years, with only a few updates required. In the long run, high-quality essentials will end up costing much less than an endless amount of fast-fashion pieces.

7 STEPS TO CREATING YOUR CAPSULE WARDROBE

So now you're convinced, but how do you go about it?

1. Start from scratch

The pursuit of personal style always begins with a clear out. Take everything out of your closet and try it on. Discard anything that doesn't fit, has never been worn, or which you hate on sight. Return the items that you're left with to your closet. If your closet is now looking too bare to, well, bear, you might want to simply buy some inexpensive basics to tide you over while you're hunting down new pieces that are more you.

2. Create an inspiration board

Much of the time, we work out what we love instinctively, by having a gut reaction to something that we've seen online, in a magazine, or on someone else. If you're not really sure what you like, an inspiration board is a great place to start. Sites like Pinterest allow you to create boards filled with looks that you like, while also letting you browse other people's boards to find even more inspiration. Gather and collate photos of the outfits and items that you like—pretty soon you should be able to start spotting common themes, which will give you a starting point when you go shopping.

3. Think about your lifestyle

One of the biggest style mistakes that people make is in shopping for an imaginary life rather than taking the time to think about the real one for which they need to dress. It's easy to fall into the trap of simply buying the clothes that you like, rather than the ones that you know you'll actually wear. It can be helpful to make a list of the kind of things that you need to dress for, and to start from there.

4. Experiment

There's a big difference between knowing what you like and knowing what suits you. You may love a particular style of dress, but find that it doesn't flatter your figure or fit in with your lifestyle. Experimenting is fun and free: you don't have to buy anything at this stage, simply try it on and take a good, long look in the mirror. Take a range of different styles into the fitting room—you might be surprised to find that the look you like best is the last thing that you would have chosen.

5. Get an objective opinion

It can be difficult to be objective when you're looking into a harshly lit fitting-room mirror, and it can also be difficult to trust the words of friends and family who don't want to hurt your feelings. Try taking a photo of your outfit—clothing can look very different on camera than it does in the mirror, and sometimes seeing a photo can completely change your opinion. It might not be easy to photograph outfits in store (a cellphone photo taken in the mirror is still better than nothing), but it's something worth trying with the clothes that you already own.

6. If it makes you feel uncomfortable, reject it

Confidence and comfort are essential components of good style. If you feel at all uncomfortable in a certain style, ditch it—no matter how good it looks.

7. Understand that it will take time to develop your personal style

It can take a lot of trial and error to arrive at a personal style that you love, and most people have plenty of fashion mishaps to look back on. Remember that style changes depending on your age, job, location, or taste. Don't be afraid to change, evolve, and experiment—not only will it help you to discover the style that works for you now, it'll also help you to understand when it's time to make a change.

SHOPPING ON A BUDGET

When it comes to shopping for your capsule wardrobe or closet essentials, one basic rule trumps all: quality over quantity.

As the whole point of the capsule is to reduce the amount of clothing that you have to buy and store, and to help you create a classic wardrobe which will last for years, many of the items that you'll find in this book are what you might think of as "investment pieces"—so they may seem expensive at first, but they'll end up costing less in the long run.

It can be helpful to think of these items on a "cost-per-wear" basis. So, a party dress that costs $50, but which you wear only once, has a cost-per-wear of $50. A high-quality leather handbag, on the other hand, might cost you $500, but if you carry it every day for years, the cost-per-wear will end up being far less than that—and probably significantly less than the $50 party dress.

While "quality over quantity" is a great idea in theory, in practice it's not always an easy one to follow. What if you can't afford those investment pieces, for instance? It's all very well telling someone that they should save up for months to buy that amazing winter coat, because it will last for years and more than earn its keep, but what if you need a coat now? What if you have a particular event to attend, and you need an outfit in a hurry? What if you've just started a new job, and need some office-appropriate outfits to wear—but you won't get paid for another month?

In all of these situations, you can't just wear nothing for months on end while you save up enough money for the perfect outfit: you either have to work with what you already have, or you simply have to settle for something that you can afford now, even if it's not the best possible quality out there. With that in mind, here are some ways to make your clothes look like they are of a higher quality than they actually are.

DON'T CONFUSE PRICE WITH QUALITY

A lot of people make the mistake of thinking that "buying quality" equals "buying designer," and that if they've spent a lot of money on an item, then it must be good quality, right? Well, not necessarily.

One of the first things that is important to understand when shopping for your capsule wardrobe is that price isn't always synonymous with quality, and you don't always get what you pay for. Rather than assuming that a high price tag equals high quality, the first rule of thumb is to buy the best quality that you can afford, which might not mean buying the most expensive item that you can find.

When you're shopping for new clothes, pay close attention to the fabric and the workmanship. Some of the cheaper brands are renowned for using low-quality fabrics, and often that reputation is deserved. Every so often, though, you'll come across a gem of an item, such as a 100 percent cashmere sweater from a popular brand, or a jacket that's so beautifully cut that no one will believe where it came from.

A lot of the time, when you're assessing the quality of an item, you can rely on touch and sight: high-quality fabrics tend to feel like they're of good quality; when you get up close to cheaper fabrics, however, you'll often notice things like shine, bobbling, or loose threads—all of which are red flags telling you that the item probably won't wash or wear well.

Natural fabrics tend to be higher quality than synthetic ones (although not always). Faux leather, for instance, can look and smell very cheap, so if you're buying leather, that's one time when you might want to save up and buy either the real thing or a high-quality imitation.

LOOK AFTER YOUR CLOTHES PROPERLY

It might seem too obvious to even mention, but one of the things that the most stylish people have in common is that they *always* look after their clothes. Even the highest-quality clothes can look cheap if you don't look after them, so iron or steam everything that needs it, replace missing buttons, polish your shoes—these things don't have to take a huge amount of time, but they'll make a big difference to how your clothes look when you wear them.

BUY CLOTHES THAT FIT

Have you ever wondered why celebrities always look immaculate, even when they're being snapped by the paparazzi, in a simple pair of jeans and a T-shirt? The answer is simple: it's because they either buy clothes that are made-to-measure or they have them tailored to fit—yes, even that white T-shirt that most of us wouldn't even consider having altered.

Of course, for those of us on a more limited budget, made-to-measure and tailoring aren't always realistic options. All the same, if you take the time to really analyze why some looks work and others don't, you'll often notice that a lot of what we consider to be perfect style comes down to a perfect fit, and when your clothes fit like they were made for you, they—and you—will look like a million dollars. Equally, you could spend a small fortune on your outfit, but if it doesn't fit you properly, you may as well have thrown that cash away, because it won't look worth the price tag.

If you can find someone who can alter your clothes on a budget that works for you, it's well worth the cost.

If you can't, it's worth shopping around a little longer, until you find something that doesn't require alterations.

KEEP IT SIMPLE

Coco Chanel once famously said that before leaving the house, you should always look in the mirror, and remove at least one piece of jewelry. While this rule might not always apply to the kind of outfits that we wear today, what Chanel was suggesting was the idea that the simplest outfits are often the most effective; and when you think of pieces like the little black dress, which Chanel popularized, it's easy to see the truth in this.

Simple lines and unfussy accessories don't just create a striking silhouette: they can also help make an outfit look more expensive than it really is. So, if you're shopping on a budget, "the simpler, the better" is a good motto to carry with you. Remember, you can always add jewelry and accessories later, if you want to add interest to the pieces that you're buying.

MAKE SMALL ALTERATIONS

We've already talked about how some "cheap" clothes can be made from surprisingly good quality fabrics, but that's not normally the case with other embellishments. One of the ways that cheaper brands save money is in details like buttons and belts, which will almost always be a much lower quality than their more expensive counterparts. Dresses from stores often come with a cheap, plastic belt; buttons tend to be flimsy ... the list goes on.

Luckily, these are quick fixes. Throw away those cheap belts—you probably already have some better quality ones in your collection, but if you don't, you can pick some up in thrift stores quite cheaply. You can also replace cheap-looking buttons with better quality ones—again, this shouldn't be too much of an investment, but it will instantly improve an outfit.

SHOP AROUND

Because you can't always assume that the price tag tells you anything about the quality of the item that you're buying, it's a good idea to shop around for the most important essentials, and to not stop looking until you've found an item that you're totally happy with. These pieces can often turn up in the most unexpected places, so don't be a style snob (or a reverse-snob, either!) and ignore certain brands or stores because you've never found anything in them before—you never know what you're going to find. Thrift stores can also be a treasure trove of clothing and accessories: a useful tip is to look for thrift stores in expensive areas of town, which often sell higher-end items at surprisingly low prices.

MIX HIGH-END WITH LOW-END

Just one quality piece can transform even the cheapest of outfits. So, a great pair of shoes will instantly elevate a cheap dress, while a quality handbag can be carried with just about anything to create a luxe look that extends to the rest of your outfit, too. You don't have to spend a lot of money on every single item that you're wearing, but the occasional investment doesn't hurt, either.

As for when to invest and when to save, well, that's largely up to you, but there are just a few items that are almost always worth investing in, if at all possible:

FIVE ITEMS OF CLOTHING THAT ARE WORTH INVESTING IN

1. Lingerie

Underwear used to be known as "foundation garments" and, although the expression itself is a little dated, it's still a good way to think about it, because underwear forms the foundation of every outfit that you wear, and can completely change the look of a garment—for better, or worse. You don't have to spend a lot of money to find underwear that fits, but do bear in mind that an ill-fitting bra, or knickers that

create lumps and bumps where you don't actually have any, can ruin the line of your clothes, or change the way that your figure looks in them. Dressing well—even if you're the only one who knows it—can be a great way to boost your confidence, which will also make you look better.

2. Workout clothes

It's easy to convince yourself that an old T-shirt and a pair of saggy leggings are fine to work out in, because who wants to spend money on something that they're just going to sweat in? This can be a false economy, though, because if you're constantly wearing and washing that old T-shirt, you're going to have to replace it much sooner than if you'd bought something that was made specifically for the job.

Not only is sportswear designed to be washed frequently without losing its shape or color, it'll also keep you cooler during your workout, thanks to the sweat-wicking fabric that most modern sportswear is made from. And it goes without saying that a supportive sports bra and pair of sneakers are well worth the investment, too.

3. Outerwear

Outerwear is one of the most frequently worn items in anyone's wardrobe, and that's particularly true for people who live in a cold climate, for whom a coat is practically an outfit in itself. For that reason, a good coat is always worth investing in—cheaper versions might look the part, but they generally won't last as long, or feel as warm. And if you're going to be wearing something every day for months on end, you're going to get your money's worth out of it!

4. Shoes and boots

While you can often find inexpensive clothing items that look just as good as their higher-end counterparts, the problem with cheap shoes is that they often look it—cheap, that is. It can be hard to resist the lure of the inexpensive ballet flat or

cheap and cheerful party shoe, but try walking a mile in those shoes first, and you'll soon realize just how much your feet will thank you for investing in something that's been well made instead.

5. Jeans

If you've ever tried to buy a new pair of jeans when your trusty old faithfuls finally wear out, then you'll know how frustrating that experience can be. For some reason, denim is one of the hardest items to find the right fit, and even if you do find jeans that fit in the waist and leg, you still have to begin the search all over again, in order to find the right wash, the right level of distressing, and so on. For this reason, when you do hit that holy grail, you're going to want to lock it down, no matter how much it costs. If you're lucky, your perfect jeans might not cost too much—store brands have made great progress with their own-brand denim over the past few years, so it's not a foregone conclusion that you're going to have to buy designer. If you do, though, be prepared to spend as much as you can reasonably invest—you won't regret it.

DRESSING FOR THE SEASONS

The real seasons don't always match the ones set by fashion designers and retailers, and it can be difficult to look a season ahead—trying to plan your summer wardrobe while it's snowing outside. Many people are moving toward a multi-season wardrobe, but how do you create a capsule that works for every season?

To move toward a capsule wardrobe that will work for you no matter what the weather throws at you, try following these practical tips:

REMEMBER: NOT ALL SEASONS ARE CREATED EQUALLY

When building a wardrobe, it's tempting to go for a 50/50 split, with half the closet dedicated to Spring/Summer and the other half to Fall/Winter. The reality is that actual seasons don't work like that: instead, ask yourself what type of clothes you wear most often. If you find yourself regularly—and optimistically—buying sundresses, but rarely get the opportunity to wear them, you're probably overestimating the length of your summer season, and need to modify your wardrobe accordingly.

ORGANIZE YOUR CLOSET TO ACCOUNT FOR SEASONAL CHANGES

An organized closet is essential. It allows you to see exactly what you have, to store items in a way that doesn't damage them, and to easily identify which clothes you do and don't wear. In an ideal world, we'd all have enough space to store every item in our capsule effortlessly, but as that's not always possible, another option is to organize your closet according to season, and to switch things around to make sure that the clothes you need now are the ones that easily come to hand. If you have sufficient storage space, you could pack your winter clothes away every spring, and vice versa. Alternatively, simply hang this season's clothes at the front/center of your closet, so that they're the most accessible.

CHOOSE LAYERING PIECES FOR ADDED VERSATILITY

If you live with unpredictable weather, you might not want to pack away a large percentage of your wardrobe every six months—an unexpected spring snowfall, and you won't have anything to wear for it. In these circumstances, layering pieces are your best friends. Cardigans, scarves, and other thin layers can be added or removed according to the temperature, and can change the look of a wardrobe basic.

DRESS FOR THE WEATHER, NOT FOR THE CALENDAR

Some people can be rigid about the concept of seasonal dressing, so they won't wear a wool coat in spring, no matter how cold it gets, and the winter clothes come out every September, even in a heatwave. Not only is this an uncomfortable way to dress, it's also not particularly stylish—no one looks good sweating under thick layers on a mild winter's day. By paying attention to the weather, rather than the calendar, you'll be able to stay comfortable and stylish, while getting maximum use out of your clothes: win-win!

DISREGARD SEASONAL-BASED RULES

"No white after Labor Day" is a popular seasonal rule (even in countries that don't actually observe this particular holiday!), while plenty of people would consider it a fashion faux pas to wear black in the height of summer. Rules, however, are made to be broken, and most of the ones relating to style are dated, with no real basis in practicality. A good rule of thumb is to think about fabric, rather than color. As a capsule wardrobe is already limited by number, there's not much to be gained by limiting the colors that you're "allowed" to wear at different times of that year—wear what works for temperature and taste instead.

VACATION PACKING

If you're wondering whether you could live with a capsule wardrobe, or if you're keen to road test one without having to commit to it full time, vacations are an excellent opportunity to put the capsule wardrobe into action.

Vacations force us, by necessity, to create a mini capsule. Lack of suitcase space will require you to think carefully about each item that you put in, and to make sure that it's going to deserve its place. As your vacation capsule will be smaller than your "real life" capsule, it can be trickier to put together. Here are some tips to get you started.

PACK AS YOU DRESS

When you're preparing for a trip, it can be easy to forget something essential. One good way to avoid this is to pack in the same order in which you'd get dressed: so, start with underwear, add in the rest of your outfit, then finish off with shoes, accessories, and any outerwear that you might need (don't forget to include nightwear). Mentally repeat this process for each day of your vacation, and you'll have at least one outfit option for each day that you'll be away from home.

CHOOSE EASY-CARE FABRICS

When you're away from home, and in the middle of a vacation, the last thing that you want to think about is finding the nearest dry cleaner, or trying to iron clothes that have been crumpled into a corner of your suitcase for the duration of a long-haul flight. Some amount of clothing care will be unavoidable, but

you can minimize the amount of time that you have to spend wielding a travel iron, or worrying about whether the hotel laundry will lose your clothes, by opting for fabrics that don't crease too easily, and which don't require specialist cleaning.

ROLL, RATHER THAN FOLD

Even the most crease-free of fabrics can look worse for wear by the end of a long flight, but rolling your clothes rather than folding them will not only mean that they'll take up less space in your suitcase (so you'll have room for shoes and accessories)—there'll be fewer creases for you to iron out at the other end, too!

CHECK THE WEATHER

It's easy to assume that your beach vacation will mean unlimited sunshine, but nothing is guaranteed in life, especially the weather, so it's a good idea to check the forecast. Even then, you never know when an unseasonable storm, or other unpredicted weather, is going to blow up, so always make sure that you have at least one "just in case" option that will work if the weather isn't quite what you expected.

PLAN FROM THE FEET UP

Footwear is never more important than when on vacation, where you're probably going to be on your feet much more than you are at home. Comfortable shoes are an absolute must, but the kind of shoes that allow you to walk for miles without getting blisters aren't always the kind that look good with that floaty dress you just threw into your suitcase. Avoid sore feet by planning all of your outfits around your most comfortable pair of shoes, and make sure that you take an extra pair with you, just in case.

USE ACCESSORIES

For shorter trips, you're probably going to want to travel light—by necessity and as a matter of convenience—which means wearing a handful of items over and over again. Even the most hardened of capsule wardrobe fans will quickly get bored when forced to wear the same outfit option every day though, which is where your accessories stash comes into play. A few well-chosen accessories can completely change the look of an outfit, and won't take up too much space. A silk scarf (see page 162), for instance, weighs next to nothing and takes up no space at all, but can be worn as a belt, headscarf, or around the neck, allowing you to get maximum mileage out of a simple cotton dress.

WEAR BULKY ITEMS ON THE PLANE

Airplanes can be subject to sudden changes in temperature, so layering is always a good idea anyway. It also allows you to take heavier items, like coats and boots, without maxing out your luggage allowance.

STYLE DOS AND DON'TS

How to be stylish? It's the million-dollar question. We may all define "style" in different ways, but most of us would (secretly or not-so-secretly) love to be stylish. It's probably the reason that you're reading this book.

You can't learn how to be stylish simply by buying the "right" clothes, or by spending a lot of money on them. Style isn't about what you buy, or about how much it costs. You can't buy style in a store, or copy it from the catwalk, and it doesn't matter how many dresses you own, or which designer name is stamped on your shoes. That's not to say that style is impossible to come by—quite the opposite, in fact. Anyone can learn how to be stylish, no matter what their budget.

DO KNOW YOUR FIGURE

Are you an apple or a pear? A rectangle or a square? It sounds like one of those silly magazine quizzes, but a large part of knowing how to be stylish is knowing what your body looks like, and then figuring out how to dress it. Remember, not all styles look good on all figures, so you have to know what you look like now—not what you'd like to look like, or how you looked ten years ago. Being brutally honest about how you look can be hard and confrontational—we all have things that we'd like to change about ourselves. Just as there's no "wrong" taste, though, there's no "wrong" shape, either. You just have to learn how to dress (and how to love) the shape that you have.

DON'T ASSUME YOU KNOW YOUR SIZE

Clothing sizes differ from brand to brand, and even from item to item, so take a range of sizes into the fitting room, and try them all on, even if you think you know which one is going to fit. While you're in the fitting room, make sure that you look at yourself from every angle (those multi-angled mirrors can be unflattering, but they're there for a reason), and take the time to move around in and sit down in the garment that you're trying on. DO buy clothes that fit (or have them altered).

How often have you seen people crammed into clothes that are clearly too small, or drowning in the excess fabric of a dress that's too big? Ill-fitting clothing is one of the fastest ways to look sloppy and unstylish, and even the most expensive clothes in the world will look bad if the fit is wrong. You might be surprised how cost-effective it can be to have a garment altered or even made from scratch. And simple alterations, such as taking up a hem or changing the length of sleeves, aren't difficult to master yourself, and will be well worth learning in the long run. The perfect fit is the holy grail of how to be stylish.

DON'T BE ASHAMED TO SIZE UP IF NECESSARY

Dress size is simply a number—and given the inconsistencies in sizing these days, not to mention the vanity-sizing that's rife throughout the fashion industry, it can be a meaningless number at that. Don't be ashamed to size up. The only person who'll know—or care—is you. The best size for you is the size that fits, regardless of the number on the label.

DON'T BE AFRAID TO "DRESS UP"

We live in a time when casual is king, and being seen to have made an effort with your appearance will often attract a lot of questions about whether you have a job interview, or have a new love interest. Life is too short not to wear the clothes that you love, and if you're going to have style-related regrets, better that they be about the clothes that you did wear—and had an absolute ball in—than the ones that hung in your closet because you were too afraid to "dress up."

DO KEEP YOUR CLOTHES CLEAN, IRONED, AND WELL-MENDED

Keep your clothes in a good state of repair, and when they get beyond repair, get rid of them. You don't need a closet full of brand new clothes to look stylish, but if your outfits look like they could walk to the bin by themselves, it might be better to let them go.

DON'T CONFUSE STYLE WITH DESIGNER LABELS

Style cannot be bought: labels can.

DO PAY ATTENTION TO DETAIL

Keep your hair clean and trimmed (if not necessarily styled to perfection), and your nails neat (you don't

need a professional manicure, just get rid of hangnails and rough edges, and keep them clean). Carefully apply makeup, and you're well on the way toward a stylish you.

DON'T BE A CLOTHES SNOB

Great items can be found in surprising places, and you never know what you might find, unless you try. Thrift stores, vintage fairs, your friend's cast-offs—all can be useful sources for original pieces.

DO KEEP IT SIMPLE

There are good reasons why some of the most stylish looks are also the simplest: think Audrey Hepburn in a pair of black capri pants and a sweater, or Marilyn's famous white dress. These outfits are easy to wear, and hard to get wrong. Accessories are a great way to update an outfit or add interest to something plain, but generally, the more elaborate your look, the easier it'll be for it to start looking messy and incoherent—the opposite of stylish.

DON'T COMPARE YOURSELF TO OTHER PEOPLE

If you want to change or improve something for your own sake, do it, but always remember that style is not a competition, and there are no prizes for copying someone else. Be yourself—everyone else is taken.

DO KNOW YOUR COMFORT LEVEL

Fashion magazines and those who live by them are always telling us to stray outside our comfort zone—to take risks, be edgy, and experiment fearlessly. Although this is worth trying from time to time (you want to be stylish, after all, not stuck in a style rut), this book is about how to be stylish, not about how to be trendy (there's an important difference). One easy way to be stylish is to know what you're comfortable wearing and, more importantly, what you're *not* comfortable wearing. Whatever you wear, it should make you feel happy, confident, and ready to take on the world.

DO DRESS APPROPRIATELY

All clothing has a context, and it's important to make sure your clothing matches the context in which it is being worn. That doesn't have to mean rigidly adhering to some imagined dress code or set of rules, however. It means not wearing sweatpants to a wedding, high heels for a walk in the countryside, a ball gown to your nephew's first birthday party, or a flimsy sundress in the snow. All of these outfits would be inappropriate for the occasion, and that means

that regardless of how good they look in their own right, they will not appear stylish.

DON'T FEEL YOU HAVE TO DRESS AGE APPROPRIATELY

If you buy fashion magazines or use Facebook, you'll frequently come across all kinds of rules relating to what women should wear at 30, 40, and onward. Most people have started to realize just how dated and irrelevant these "rules" are, and to completely disregard them, as they should. There's no magic cut-off point at which it suddenly becomes inappropriate to wear a certain item—that miniskirt will look exactly the same on your 30th birthday as it did the day before, when you were still 29. The only real answer to the question, "How old is too old for … ?" is, "When it no longer looks good, or when you no longer feel good in it."

DO REGULARLY AUDIT YOUR CLOSET

Although you don't have to change your look based on arbitrary rules, age-based or otherwise, few people will want to wear the same styles for their entire lives, and it's important not to get stuck in a rut, buying the same things without ever questioning them or trying something different. Go through your closet a couple of times a year and take stock of what you've been wearing on repeat and what's been languishing in the corner, unloved. As well as refining your personal style, you'll also be able to change it as required, by identifying items that aren't working for you and looking for new styles to replace them.

DON'T FOLLOW A TREND, UNLESS YOU LOVE IT

Fashion can be fun, but when it comes to style, it's always better to buy clothes simply because you like them, not because you think you *should* like them, or because you know they're "on trend." You don't have to follow fashion, dress down because everyone else does, or force yourself to wear clothes that you don't feel comfortable in.

CLOTHING CARE

You could go out and buy the best quality clothing in the world, but unless you know how to look after it properly, it still won't look stylish. Here are some ways to look after your clothes, to make sure that they look as good as possible, for as long as possible.

THE DON'TS

Don't try to live a dry-clean lifestyle on a machine-wash budget

You find something that you love, but it's dry clean only, and you know that you're not going to visit the cleaners every couple of weeks, let alone pay for regular cleaning. It'll be okay if you hand-wash it, or machine-wash it on a low temperature, right? WRONG. While some "dry clean only" clothing can be cleaned carefully at home, if the item is expensive, don't risk it. Find machine- or hand-washable alternatives.

Don't over-wash your clothes

While some clothes (underwear, sports clothes, etc.) need to be washed after every use, others don't, especially if you're not sweating while you wear them. As a guide, if it's not in direct contact with your skin, it should only need to be washed when it looks or smells dirty.

Don't overfill your washing machine

Cramming your washing machine might cut down on the number of loads you have to do, but it's an easy way to ruin your clothes, prevent them getting clean, and it'll take longer to iron them.

Try not to tumble

Often it's not washing clothes that's the problem—it's drying them. Tumble drying can be tough on clothing, particularly on delicate fabrics, so try to let things air-dry whenever possible. Delicates should always be laid out flat and allowed to dry naturally.

THE DOS

Always read the label

How often do you take the time to read the care label before tossing that precious garment into the laundry? Many people don't bother, and simply assume that they know how their clothes should be cleaned—but the instructions are there for a reason, so read them!

Separate items

Don't be tempted to cut down on laundry by throwing everything in the machine together. That's an easy way to end up with dingy gray panties—not a great look! Separate colors from whites and easy-care items from delicates.

Buy a laundry bag

A mesh laundry bag will enable you to wash delicates like lingerie without worrying about them getting ruined. (Warning: If they're super-delicate or hand-wash only, DON'T put them in the machine, even in a laundry bag!) If you don't have a laundry bag, however, a pillowcase will also work.

Use the coolest temperature possible

It might seem like a good idea to get everything clean by washing it at heat, but seriously, it's not. It's just a good way to ruin things or wear them out faster. Use the coolest temperature that you can get away with—it's better to have to wash it again if that stain doesn't shift than to ruin the garment.

Wash jeans and other over-dyed items inside out

Dark-wash jeans will fade super-fast if you wash them too often, or on too hot a temperature. If possible, it's best to try and hand-wash those items in cool water. If machine-washing, turn them inside out to help prevent fading.

If you have to tumble, add tennis balls!

Wrap a few tennis balls in a sock (to avoid infecting your laundry with yellow fuzz), add them to your tumble dryer, and it will reduce drying time while also prolonging the life of your clothes.

Spot-clean rather than clean-clean

If stains are the problem, try using a stain-removal pen to get rid of them rather than washing the entire item.

Wear a slip

If you wear a lot of skirts or dresses, not only will a silk slip make them look better when worn, it'll also prevent oil from the skin getting on to your clothes.

You will need to wash the slip itself frequently, but rather that than over-washing your dresses.

Iron with care

If you can get away without ironing certain items, go for it (lying items flat to dry, or carefully hanging them, can help creases to drop out). If you can't, use your iron on the lowest heat possible, and try placing a thin pillowcase or other piece of fabric on top of delicate fabrics to avoid scorching them.

DRESSES AND SKIRTS

FULL SKIRT

Beloved of fashion bloggers and 1950s debutantes alike, the full skirt is one of those styles that some people find a little daunting. Worry not—style should never be scary. (Repeat after me: "It's just a skirt.") There are plenty of ways to make this style work for modern life. Skipping the petticoat is one of them: when Christian Dior popularized the full skirt as part of his New Look in the late 40s, it was at a time when women thought nothing of adding layers of crinoline under their clothes, and wouldn't have dreamt of going out without gloves and a hat.

Although today's full skirts might echo the feminine style of a bygone age, they stop short of outright copying it, which will be a relief for anyone who's ever tried to do the grocery shop or drive a car wearing a crinoline and heels, and realized too late that those classic styles need tweaking to work with today's lifestyles.

SEE ALSO
Sweatshirt, p. 94
Denim Jacket, p. 102

1. KNOTTED SHIRT Give a nod to the 50s with a knotted shirt—just keep makeup and hair subtle, to avoid looking like an extra from *Grease*.

2. SWEATSHIRT A casual sweatshirt might not be the obvious match for a dressy skirt, but it's an easy way to create a contemporary look from what can be a traditional style.

3. T-SHIRT AND SANDALS A full skirt is an airy, floaty choice for warmer weather—just add sandals and accessories, as appropriate.

4. DENIM JACKET AND BRETON A denim jacket and striped top is one of those classic pairings that work with everything, including dressing down a full skirt for a relaxed weekend look.

5. SWEATER AND BAG Go for head-to-toe black, red, green, or whatever your choice of color, for a smart, coordinated style, with maximum silhouette-defining impact.

A-LINE SKIRT

It's not hard to work out why the A-line skirt is so-called: the term refers to any skirt, long or short, which creates that distinctive letter "A" silhouette, with a defined waist flaring out over the hips. The term "A-line," however, can be used to describe a wide variety of skirts, from super-short minis to floor-length maxis—and everything in between—making it one of the more versatile skirt styles you'll find.

Because the A-line shape works for most body types, the skirts tend to be readily available in stores regardless of the season. Hem lengths, colors, and patterns might change to fit current trends, but the A-line skirt will probably always be in fashion, in one form or another.

SEE ALSO
Dressy Top, p. 78
White Sneakers, p. 146

HOW TO WEAR IT

1   2   3   4   5

1. EVENING HEELS A structured A-line skirt can easily be dressed up for evenings, with the addition of statement pieces such as jewelry or a great pair of heels. Look for luxe fabrics like silk or cashmere on top, to complete the look.

2. OFF-THE-SHOULDER TOP AND SANDALS Shorter A-line skirts are perfect for summer vacations, as they can be easily dressed up or down as required. For a day's sightseeing or café-hopping, add a floaty off-the-shoulder top and flat sandals.

3. SNEAKERS AND SHIRT Give an A-line skirt a more casual feel by pairing with classic sneakers and an oversized shirt, for a wear-anywhere look.

4. HEELS, CLUTCH, AND TOP Make your summer skirt do double-duty as wedding guest attire by wearing it with heels, a clutch, and a dressy top.

5. CARDIGAN AND TIGHTS The simple shape of an A-line skirt works well for the office, just add tights and a cardigan to beat the winter chill.

MINISKIRT

Think of the miniskirt and you will probably think of someone like Twiggy—all legs, eyelashes, and effortless 60s cool. The miniskirt was born in that era, and whether it was created by Mary Quant or André Courrèges (both claim the crown), the end result is the same: a short skirt designed to show off the legs, skim the thigh, and scandalize teachers and parents, who have spent decades engaged in a fruitless battle against the ever-shortening hemline.

The mini is here to stay, though, and although most of us can only dream of having legs like Twiggy, the good news is that the mini can help us fake it: that short hem makes legs look longer, which is one of the main reasons for its popularity. To classify as a true mini, your skirt should end no more than four inches below the buttocks. As no one's going to be measuring your hem, though, you can easily go a little longer (or shorter) without losing the look. Some people swear by the "fingertip rule," which states that your skirt should at least reach the tips of your fingers when your arms are down by your sides.

SEE ALSO

Turtleneck Sweater, p. 88
Slouchy Sweater, p. 98

1   2   3   4   5

1. SNEAKERS AND SWEATSHIRT
For instant sport chic, just add sneakers and a sweatshirt.

2. CARDIGAN AND TIGHTS
Short skirts won't be appropriate for all workplaces, but by wearing yours with tights and layering a cardigan over a smarter top, a mini can easily work for more casual offices.

3. SLOUCHY SWEATER
Play with proportions with an oversized, slouchy sweater to balance out a shorter, dressier skirt.

4. ANKLE BOOTS AND TURTLENECK
Give a nod to 60s style with a turtleneck sweater, but keep the look contemporary with ankle boots.

5. LONGLINE CARDIGAN AND FLATS
Layer up a tailored skirt with confidence—patent flats, a crisp shirt, and a longline cardigan, which looks smart enough for an interview—even if the skirt is short!

PENCIL SKIRT

Created by Christian Dior, and designed to make women walk with a "wiggle" (which is why they're often referred to as "wiggle skirts"), the pencil skirt offers a shortcut to grown-up glamour and ladylike style. The straight-cut skirt is designed to hug the hips and fall to just below the knee—and don't worry, today's styles won't necessarily cause you to wiggle, thanks to stretch fabrics and more forgiving cuts.

These days, the office is the pencil skirt's natural habitat, and it forms the basis of many a working wardrobe, pairing easily with blazers and shirts to create a polished, professional style. The inherent glamour of the style makes it a natural choice for eveningwear, too, which is why a black (or other block color) pencil skirt is such an essential in many women's closets.

SEE ALSO
Ballet Flats, p. 136
Leather Belt, p. 160

1   2   3   4   5

1. BLAZER AND PUMPS The pencil skirt is a workwear staple, which is perfect with a blazer and pumps—two other office staples.

2. SWEATER AND BOOTS A slouchy sweater and ankle boots create that effortless, "model off duty" look when paired with a simple pencil skirt.

3. BELT AND SWEATER Go for a pinup-inspired look by wearing a bodycon skirt with a wide belt and fitted sweater.

4. BLOUSE Try a retro-inspired look by wearing a pussy-bow blouse with a knee-length pencil skirt. It's very "70s secretary," but in a stylish way.

5. TANK TOP AND HEELS A brightly colored tank top instantly adds a modern edge to a pencil skirt—just add killer heels to complete the look.

PLEATED SKIRT

If your school had a strict uniform, your memories of pleated skirts worn with knee-high socks and "sensible" shoes might not exactly encourage you to want to give pleats a space in your closet ever again. If that's the case, then take a deep breath and give pleats a chance: they've been going through an unexpected renaissance recently, and today's pleated skirts are a world away from the ones that you might have grudgingly worn to school—or, at least, they can be, if you style them the right way.

There's no denying, however, that pleats can be problematic—they can make hips look wider than they are, and give volume to places where you don't need or want it. But, worn right, pleated skirts can also be either floaty and feminine, or cool and edgy. In addition, today's skirts come in shimmering hues of silver and gold, as well as in a rainbow of different colors.

SEE ALSO
Slouchy Sweater, p. 98
Clutch Bag, p. 152

1   2   3   4   5

1. T-SHIRT AND SNEAKERS Pleated skirts can feel (and look) very prim and proper. Sneakers, on the other hand, usually don't, so put the two together, team with an oversized tee, and enjoy a dressed-down take on pleats.

2. STRAPPY SANDALS If your skirt is midi-length or longer, heels are essential to help avoid the "frump factor" that pleats can bring to an outfit.

3. NECKLACE AND CLUTCH
Play up the ladylike feel of a pleated skirt by accessorizing with a statement necklace and clutch bag, perfect for a summer event.

4. BOOTS AND CARDIGAN
Pleats can make a nice alternative to a pencil skirt for the office: knee-high boots and a sweater or heavy wool cardigan will take your skirt sashaying into the winter season.

5. SLOUCHY SWEATER AND HAT
A slouchy sweater and felt hat gives a contemporary country feel to an otherwise traditional look.

OFFICE DRESS

The words "office dress" might bring to mind the set of *Mad Men*, awash with wiggle dresses and high heels, but as today's workplaces tend to be a little less formal (and hopefully a lot less sexist), it's probably easier to define what an office dress *isn't* rather than what it is.

An office dress generally isn't too short, too tight, or too revealing. It's not the kind of dress that you'd wear to go clubbing, or to go to the beach—and it's not the kind of dress you'd wear to a wedding, either. Take out all of the dresses in your closet which fit that description, and what you're left with is probably office-appropriate.

Of course, it's worth pointing out here that all offices are different, so what's fine for one office might raise a few eyebrows in the one next door. The best advice? Look at the clothes that your female bosses wear, and take your cue from them.

SEE ALSO
Denim Jacket, p. 102
Silk Scarf, p. 162

1   2   3   4   5

1. COTTON SHIRT Give your dress a menswear-inspired vibe by layering a shirt underneath.

2. NECK SCARF AND BALLET FLATS Pair a chic neck scarf with a classic shift dress and flats for a timeless look that will never go out of style.

3. DENIM JACKET Who says that your office dress has to stay in the office? Make it work overtime by wearing it with a denim jacket after hours.

4. LONGLINE CARDIGAN Soft, drapey knits are a good way to soften up an all-business look.

5. FITTED CARDIGAN A cute fitted cardigan sitting on the hips is the perfect length to add waistline definition.

SUMMER DRESS

When it's hot and sticky outside, the last thing that you want to do is spend time fussing with a complicated outfit. Enter the sundress: the ultimate in simple, summer dressing, this is a lightweight dress, normally made from cotton, which is designed to keep you cool and comfortable, no matter how warm it gets. Sundresses are designed to be worn as standalone pieces, so they don't require much in the way of accessorizing or styling, which makes them an easy choice for those days when you just want to get dressed and go outside.

Sundresses come in all shapes and sizes, and although their designers tend to favor light, bright colors (thought to be cooler to wear than darker shades), you'll find them in a wide variety of colors and prints, making it easy enough to find one to suit your style and shape.

SEE ALSO

White Sneakers, p. 146
Hat, p. 166

1   2   3   4   5

1. BELT AND HEELS Take your sundress from day to night by adding a great pair of heels, plus accessories like belts and jewelry to dress it up even more.

2. KNOTTED SHIRT Although you might not think of a sundress as natural office attire, by wearing it as a skirt, with a shirt or sweater on top, you can easily make your dress do double duty.

3. HAT A wide-brimmed sunhat is the perfect accessory for a simple dress, and it'll protect your scalp from sunburn, too.

4. SNEAKERS Give a laidback vibe to a short sundress by donning your white sneakers.

5. CARDIGAN AND NECKLACE Although sundresses tend to be fairly casual, a cute cardigan and statement necklace will dress one up when required, and help you to wear your dress even when the sun is reluctant to shine.

WRAP DRESS

When you see the words "wrap dress" in a fashion magazine, they're almost always accompanied by the words "universally flattering." This simple, wrap-around dress, popularized by Diane Von Furstenberg in the 1970s, is lauded for its ability to be dressed up or down, and to suit every shape: but here's a little-known secret—it doesn't.

There's no such thing as a "one size fits all" solution, and while the wrap dress will work for many women, it does require some thought. The deep V-shaped neckline, for instance, might require a cami or slip underneath if you don't want it to be too revealing; the clingy, jersey fabric that these dresses are typically made from can highlight lumps and bumps. But if you're looking for an easy-to-wear dress that will take you just about anywhere, the wrap dress is worth a shot.

SEE ALSO

Silk Cami, p. 72
Hat, p. 166

1   2   3   4   5

1. BLAZER AND CAMI Wrap dresses can be a little low cut for some tastes, but by layering a camisole underneath and a blazer on top, you can easily keep the look professional.

2. VEST Add a longline vest or cardigan for a smart/casual daytime look.

3. BOHO HAT Give a nod to the era in which the wrap dress was created, with a 70s-style wide-brimmed hat.

4. SNEAKERS AND SHIRT Keep things simple with classic sneakers and an open denim shirt layered over your dress.

5. SATCHEL AND FLATS Choose a summery print and fabric, pack your best matching satchel and flats, don your cutest sunglasses, and take yourself off for a day's sightseeing in comfort and style.

LITTLE BLACK DRESS

Everyone's heard of the little black dress (or LBD, for short), but not everyone knows where it came from. Audrey Hepburn wore one, and black is the color Coco Chanel used when she popularized the dress back in the 1920s. The real key to the LBD's success, however, lies in its simplicity, rather than its color.

The LBD is your wardrobe workhorse. It's the dress that you wear to work, and then out to drinks afterward, and it's also the dress that you wear on the weekend, purely because it makes you feel fantastic every time you put it on. For a dress to be this versatile, it has to be simply cut and in a neutral color that will work with everything else in your closet, as well as with your coloring and personal style. If black isn't your color (and contrary to popular opinion, it doesn't work for everyone), other neutrals like navy, forest green, or gray can work just as well. The most important thing is that the dress is in a block color, rather than patterned.

SEE ALSO

Heavy Wool Cardigan, p. 92
Clutch Bag, p. 152

1   2   3   4   5

1. CASUAL CARDIGAN The LBD doesn't have to be reserved for office wear or eveningwear—throw on a chunky cardi and a pair of ankle boots for a casual, weekend look.

2. SPORTY SNEAKERS Sporty doesn't have to mean sloppy. Team a casual LBD with sneakers and a baseball cap for a sassy, preppy look.

3. HEELS AND CLUTCH Heels and a clutch bag will always create a classic evening look when worn with a black dress. A belt and contrasting shoes, however, will create more interest, and allow you to give the look some personality.

4. BOOTS AND SCARF Flat boots and a colored or printed scarf will instantly give a boho feel to a black bodycon dress.

5. TALL BOOTS AND COAT Play with proportions by layering a long coat over a short black dress and then adding a pair of tall boots. As long as the coat is longer than the dress, this chic look will work.

PRINTED DRESS

If single-color dresses are the sensible and sophisticated workhorses of your closet, then printed dresses are their slightly more fun younger sister. That's not to say that prints can't be sophisticated or sensible, of course (or that block colors can't be fun, for that matter), but while a single-color dress is probably the more versatile option, prints offer a great opportunity to inject some personality into your outfits.

For some people, bold prints featuring lots of colors can seem daunting. The great thing about printed dresses, however, is that they're an entire outfit in themselves—and as long as you keep the rest of your look simple, they can be easier to wear than you might think.

SEE ALSO

Strappy Heels, p. 148
Hat, p. 166

1   2   3   4   5

1. LONGLINE CARDIGAN AND TIGHTS They may be most often associated with spring and summer, but printed dresses can be layered up with chunky knitwear and cozy, colorful tights for the cooler seasons, too.

2. BAG, HAT, AND SOCKS For a more bohemian take on the printed dress, look for fringed bags, wide-brimmed hats, and knee-length socks.

3. BELT AND ACCESSORIES Florals will never go out of style for summer—and with good reason. Use a belt to cinch the waist of a flowing dress, and add tan leather accessories, which will work with any color combination and pattern.

4. ANKLE SOCKS AND BACKPACK If a printed dress feels way too "ladylike" (read: dull) to you, unexpected touches like ankle socks and utilitarian accessories can make all the difference.

5. STRAPPY SANDALS Floral dresses can seem very demure, but a pair of high, strappy sandals will give more impact with a sophisticated twist.

SKATER DRESS

If the words "skater dress" make you think of the kind of short, satin dresses that figure skaters wear, you're only partly right. Skater dresses are, indeed, named after the dresses that you might see on the ice, but don't worry: the ones that you'll find in stores are much less flamboyant—and there are no tan pantyhose required!

Outside the world of competitive ice dancing, the term "skater" is used to refer to a style of dress that's fitted to the waist, flaring out into a circle skirt. For this reason, skater dresses are also often known as "fit and flare" dresses, and they come in a variety of different lengths, ranging from the tiniest mini to the more sophisticated midi. Because of the wide range of styles available, skater dresses are popular and show no signs of going out of fashion, making them a hard-working addition to any wardrobe.

SEE ALSO

Heavy Wool Cardigan, p. 92
Ankle Boots, p. 144

1   2   3   4   5

1. SWEATER Make sure that your short-sleeved dress survives the winter season by layering with a fine-knit sweater underneath for added warmth.

2. TIGHTS When wearing a short dress to work, neutral tights—especially black— are an easy way to carry the look into the professional arena.

3. BLAZER AND HEELS For evenings and special events, you can always rely on heels and a blazer to dress up an item.

4. LONGLINE CARDIGAN A long, floaty cardigan adds a romantic feel to a structured skater dress.

5. ANKLE BOOTS AND CARDIGAN Toughen up a floral skater dress with a pair of leather ankle boots and a chunky-knit cardigan.

COCKTAIL DRESS

How many times have you been invited to a party and immediately started panicking because you have absolutely nothing to wear? That's why your closet needs a cocktail dress. This dress is the one that you'll wear to any occasion with a formal dress code: so, all of those invitations that drop into your mailbox and send you into a spiral of sartorial despair, basically.

Less formal—and shorter—than an evening gown, the cocktail dress is still going to be one of the dressier items that you own, so it's likely to be made from a luxe-look fabric, like satin or lace, and may have some form of embellishment, such as beading or embroidery. Black is popular, due to its versatility (you can wear the same black cocktail dress to multiple events, styling it differently each time), but other colors are equally acceptable. The dress can be fitted or flared, strapless or sleeved, and with endless different details. Hems generally hit around knee-length, but longer and shorter versions aren't unusual.

SEE ALSO

Denim Jacket, p. 102
Clutch Bag, p. 152

HOW TO WEAR IT

1   2   3   4   5

1. TAILORED JACKET Rather than
allowing a special dress to be a "wear once
wonder," try layering a fitted jacket over
the top and wearing it to work.

2. DENIM JACKET AND SANDALS
Although it's tempting to view cocktail
dresses as being reserved for special
occasions, a classic dress can be dressed
down with a denim jacket and sandals,
making your wardrobe work hard for you.

3. EVENING BELT Colorful accessories
with allow you to stamp your personality
on a plain shift dress, as well as changing
the look of the outfit to suit your mood.

4. OCCASION SHAWL Fancy detailing
gives a knee-length cocktail dress added
interest, while a chiffon shawl will let you
cover up, without dressing down.

5. SHRUG AND CLUTCH BAG
For the dressiest of occasions, a luxe
clutch bag is the perfect pairing for a
classic cocktail dress. If you don't want to
bare your upper arms, a shrug or bolero
over your dress is a stylish solution.

KNIT
DRESS

Even the most stylish women out there can struggle to retain their sense of style when winter rolls around. The colder months of the year can make it tempting to take refuge in jeans, sweaters, and as many layers as possible—which is where the knit dress comes in.

The knit dress (or "sweater dress") doesn't have to be nearly as casual as the name suggests. While some variations do take the form of a very long sweater, making them a great informal option, fine-knit dresses can be a little more elegant, and wouldn't be out of place in the office or on an evening out.

Of course, as the only real requirement of this style is that the dress in question be made of a knit fabric (normally some kind of wool or cashmere blend), there are endless options available, making it one of those style saviors that you'll be glad you stocked up on when you're staring down the barrel of another cold day.

SEE ALSO
Black Leggings, p. 122
Wedge Heels, p. 140

1   2   3   4   5

1. SCARF AND HIGH BOOTS Layer up your woolens for a smart/casual look that's as chic as it is cozy.

2. BLAZER AND BELT A fine-knit dress can still be professional enough for the office: just add your trusty blazer and a stylish belt to add interest and shape.

3. LEGGINGS The laidback style of sweater dresses makes them the perfect choice with leggings, for a look that's as comfortable as it is cute.

4. WEDGES A knit dress might not seem like the obvious choice for a summer vacation, but a cold-shoulder cut and lighter weight of knit can add versatility to this style.

5. HEELED SANDALS If you don't want to look overdressed, try pairing a slouchy dress with a pair of strappy heels for an easy, evening look.

TOPS
AND
SHIRTS

WHITE SHIRT

"When I don't know what to wear, it's what I choose," said fashion designer Carolina Herrera, backstage at one of her shows. She was speaking, of course, about the white shirt, and she's not the only stylish woman to sing its praises. Katharine Hepburn, Marilyn Monroe, and Grace Kelly all viewed the white shirt as the epitome of off-duty style, and it's one item that looks just as good today as it did back in its Hollywood heyday.

White shirts are often associated with uniforms, but they can be the ultimate in casual chic, making their wearer look effortlessly polished without being overdone. For many women, they're still a uniform of sorts, but not the kind that you might normally associate with that word.

SEE ALSO

A-Line Skirt, p. 42
Sunglasses, p. 164

1   2   3   4   5

1. SUMMER SKIRT You might think of it primarily as office wear, but take your white shirt on vacation—along with your flowing floral skirt or dress—and wear it knotted at the waist as an easy cover-up.

2. A-LINE SKIRT This is one of those no-effort combinations that always looks like it took way more effort than it actually did—perfect for formal occasions.

3. LONG SKIRT What would office workers do without white shirts? Give the work uniform a more contemporary feel by wearing your shirt tucked into a high-waisted, long-length skirt.

4. JEANS AND SUNGLASSES Blue jeans, white shirt—not just a Lana Del Rey song, but also the kind of outfit that you just can't go wrong with. Hang your sunglasses from the top of your shirt to look even more laidback.

5. CROPPED SWEATER AND HEELS Make your black jeans evening-appropriate by teaming them with a crisp white shirt under a cropped sweater, and pair with killer heels.

DENIM SHIRT

If you think denim shirts are for cowboys and country singers, you're … well, you're partly right: the hardwearing fabric does have its origins in the American West, with cattle-herders adopting it as a uniform of choice (the country singers came later), but nowadays you're just as likely to see denim shirts on the backs of clotheshorses as you are on real ones.

If denim doesn't quite do it for you, chambray is its lighter-weight sister. Made from fabrics like cotton or linen, chambray looks similar to denim, but is a little easier to wear, especially in warmer months, when heavy denim might feel restrictive.

Whether your shirt is chambray or denim, it's a true workhorse, which can be layered under knitwear or worn on its own as a casual companion for jeans, pants, and skirts. Just avoid the rhinestones, unless you're channeling your inner Dolly Parton.

▶ **SEE ALSO**

White Jeans, p. 126
Flat Sandals, p. 134

1   2   3   4   5

1. SHORTS, SANDALS, AND SUNHAT On warmer days, roll up your shirt sleeves and wear your denim shirt with shorts, sandals, and sun hat—a vacation classic.

2. JEANS If you're wary of committing a "double denim" style crime, use two contrasting shades of the fabric.

3. SUMMER DRESS A denim shirt makes a useful summer night's cover-up: just tie it around your waist when you're not wearing it.

4. BLACK PANTS AND BLAZER Breathe new life into your office uniform by switching your white shirt for a denim one.

5. WHITE TEE AND PANTS Your natural inclination might be to layer a shirt under a sweater, but heavier denim can function as a lightweight jacket when worn open, over the top of a T-shirt or a long-sleeved top.

SILK CAMI

Camisole tops might have started life as lingerie or nightwear, but they're a mainstay of the modern capsule closet, and much too pretty to stay hidden underneath your clothes. The modern cami can be defined as any top with thin, spaghetti-style straps and a fairly loose shape that skims the contours of the body rather than clinging to them. It's the silk cami that's normally cited as a closet essential, and with good reason: when it comes to luxury, there's nothing quite like silk, and it's a touch more special than fabrics like cotton or spandex, which are generally used for vest and tank tops.

Although a silk top might seem like an inevitably dressy option, one of the reasons that these tops made the leap from lingerie to everyday wear is down to their sheer versatility—a cami top will dress up a pair of jeans, with the lace or beaded embellishments that are often found on these tops making them a great option for eveningwear, too.

SEE ALSO

Miniskirt, p. 44
Trench Coat, p. 110

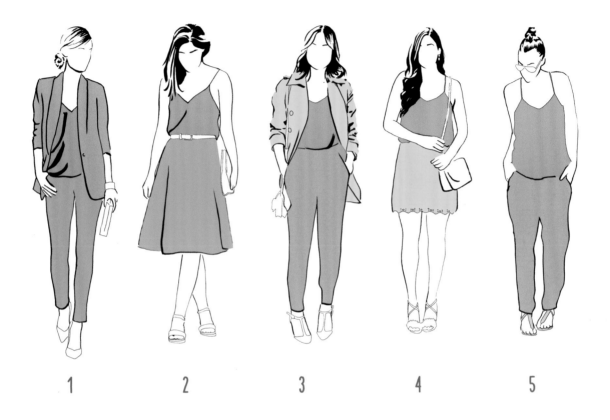

1   2   3   4   5

1. BLAZER AND SKINNIES Bring all of your hardest-working essentials together in one look: the combination of blazer, cami, jeans, and heels is one you just can't go wrong with!

2. A-LINE SKIRT A flowing skirt creates a sophisticated, unstructured look when paired with a silk camisole.

3. TRENCH AND TAILORED PANTS A cami top gives a luxe look to a pair of tailored pants, while a classic trench coat completes the look.

4. MINISKIRT The silk cami is the ultimate evening-out top, as it's dressy without being too fussy, which means that you can wear it with just about anything.

5. RELAXED PANTS AND SANDALS When you don't want your basics to look too basic, swap your cotton tank for a silk camisole, and look instantly more pulled together.

WHITE T-SHIRT

There are lots of items of clothing which are said to "look good on everyone," but the humble white T-shirt is one of the few pieces that actually does. Not bad for a piece of clothing that started out as men's underwear!

The white T-shirt has come a long way since then, though, and although some might consider it too dull for words, it's the very simplicity of the white tee that's the key to its success. This is a garment that can truly be anything that you want it to be: it's easily incorporated into just about any outfit, and although it's often described as iconic, it's the piece that lets the rest of the outfit—or the person wearing it—shine. It would be hard to imagine *Rebel Without a Cause* without James Dean in his white T-shirt, after all— the ultimate proof that clothes don't have to be complicated (or expensive) to be memorable.

SEE ALSO
Miniskirt, p. 44
Wide-Leg Pants, p. 130

1   2   3   4   5

1. PENCIL SKIRT AND HEELS

A white T-shirt might not be the first thing that you'd think of when it comes to eveningwear, but try it with a pencil skirt and heels, and you might just be surprised by the result.

2. WIDE-LEG PANTS AND BLAZER

The clean lines of a white T-shirt make it a good choice for smart/casual office attire: wear with wide-leg pants and a blazer to keep the look sharp and current.

3. SUMMER PANTS

For sheer simplicity and a classic summer look that will never tire, team your white tee with loose, cropped pants—choose a subtle print for added interest.

4. FULL SKIRT

When your skirt (or pants) have a loud or busy print, a plain white tee will allow the print to stand out, rather than competing with it.

5. MINISKIRT

The shorter the hem, the higher the neckline—making a T-shirt the perfect pairing for a miniskirt.

BRETON TOP

Who would've thought that the uniform of the French navy would one day become the uniform of stylish women the world over? "Uniform" is the right word, too: for many women, a striped top of some description (the original Bretons had twenty-one stripes, one for each of Napoleon's victories, but today the term is used to describe any kind of stripe) is the ultimate closet essential, worn with everything from the most casual pair of jeans imaginable to the fanciest of skirts. There's something about stripes that conveys an air of effortless cool, which is probably why the Breton top has become the off-duty uniform of ... well, almost everyone.

While the classic Breton mixes blue and white stripes, today's tops come in a variety of colors, from the nautical reds, whites, and blues, which are most associated with the style, to greens, yellows, and pinks.

SEE ALSO

Pencil Skirt, p. 46
White Shirt, p. 68

1   2   3   4   5

1. TAILORED PANTS There are few looks more classic than the pairing of Breton stripes with tailored pants: the perfect smart/casual look.

2. A-LINE SKIRT AND FLATS Take your stripes to work by teaming them with an A-line skirt and pointed flats, for an informal office look with a touch of polish.

3. PRINTED PENCIL SKIRT Mixing prints doesn't always work, but one pairing that's easy to pull off is stripes and florals— you might be surprised by just how good it looks.

4. JEANS AND SHIRT A Breton and jeans is the weekend uniform of many, but mix it up a bit by wearing your Breton as a sweater over the top of a thin shirt.

5. SKINNY JEANS AND JACKET Add a tailored jacket to your skinnies and Breton, and statement accessories to make the outfit more evening appropriate.

DRESSY TOP

"Jeans and a nice top"—how often have you heard that particular answer to the question, "So, what are you going to wear tonight?" Okay, so it might be a little predictable (it's basically the fallback going-out uniform of choice for women who don't know what to wear), but there's no denying that it's a handy formula to have in reserve, as are the "nice" tops that form such an integral part of it.

Of course, you don't always have to wear your nice top with a pair of jeans. The beauty of the dressy top is that it'll do exactly as the name implies, and make just about anything look instantly dressy. As for the top itself, there are too many options to count, but the type of tops most often referred to in this way tend to have some kind of fancier-than-usual element to them: sequins, lace, embroidery, an off-the-shoulder neckline, or a strapless design.

SEE ALSO
Wide-Leg Pants, p. 130
Ankle Boots, p. 144

1   2   3   4   5

1. TAILORED PANTS AND FLATS
That fancy top you wore out on the town will also work for the office, with tapered trousers and leather flats.

2. SHORTS AND FLATS You'll never run out of uses for a neutral dressy top on vacation—it'll look just as good with pleated shorts and flat shoes during the day as with a skirt and heels in the evening.

3. WIDE-LEG PANTS For a change from wearing skirts or dresses to special occasions, try pairing a lace or sequined top with wide-leg pants instead. It's a modern look, which is still dressy enough for a wedding or party.

4. CROPPED SKINNIES Casual doesn't always have to mean basic—by switching your usual T-shirt or sweater for a dressy top, you'll add interest without losing the casual feel.

5. MINISKIRT AND ANKLE BOOTS
A dressy top will work with just about everything, and is the perfect way to offset a leather miniskirt and ankle boots, for a night out.

SILK BLOUSE

What's the difference between a silk shirt and a silk blouse? In general terms, the word "shirt" can be used to describe almost any garment worn on the top half of the body, whereas blouse normally refers to button-down garments with cuffs and a collar. When it comes to the silk shirt, the lines are even blurrier, with both terms being used almost interchangeably. So, while all silk blouses are essentially shirts, albeit often with a slightly looser, less structured cut, not all shirts are blouses.

Confused? Don't be—because it's not really the cut, or the buttons, or the shape of the collar that makes the silk shirt or blouse such a classic—it's that beautiful silk fabric, which flows over the body, and gives the garment its touch of luxury and elegance.

SEE ALSO

Miniskirt, p. 44
Pleated Skirt, p. 48

1   2   3   4   5

1. MINISKIRT A silk blouse adds sophistication to a leather skirt: the unstructured top helps to balance out the tight, shorter skirt, while the silk fabric softens the look.

2. SLIM PANTS AND TOTE Button-downs are a staple of many people's professional wardrobes, but choosing silk rather than cotton makes the outfit feel less like a uniform.

3. LOOSE PANTS Choose loose pants and leather accessories for an effortless, drapey, smart/casual look.

4. JEANS AND SHOES Tuck your silk shirt into vintage blue jeans and team with strikingly bright-colored shoes for the ultimate in casual luxury—don't forget your clutch and sunglasses!

5. PLEATED SKIRT A pleated maxi skirt worn with a loose silk blouse creates a glamorous, slightly bohemian look for summer evenings.

BLACK TANK TOP

Tank top, sleeveless shirt—this garment has many names, but you probably won't have too much trouble recognizing it: in fact, chances are that you have at least one of these lurking somewhere in your closet already. As for whether or not you'd describe your trusty black tank top as a "fashion statement," well, you probably wouldn't. That's okay, though, because the tank top was never supposed to be high fashion. The very first "tanks" were the one-piece bathing costumes that women wore to the pool, or "swimming tank," in the 1920s.

Now, the tank top is another one of those building-block items that forms the basis of countless other outfits: while it may not be the most interesting item that you'll ever buy, it could well be one of the most versatile.

▶ **SEE ALSO**

Full Skirt, p. 40
Cropped Cardigan, p. 96

1 2 3 4 5

1. FULL SKIRT A simple black tank will look effortlessly chic when paired with a classic full skirt for the evening.

2. CROPPED CARDIGAN AND PENCIL SKIRT It would be too informal to wear on its own, but layer a cute, cropped cardigan over your basic black tank and wear it with a pencil skirt to the office.

3. LEGGINGS, BOOTS, AND BIKER JACKET Wear a longline tank top over leggings for a comfortable, casual look, which is instantly toughened and warmed up by a biker jacket and boots.

4. SKINNY JEANS AND SANDALS Skinny jeans and sandals create a streamlined, laidback summer look when worn with a sleeveless top.

5. BOYFRIEND JEANS The casual nature of the tank top works well with boyfriend jeans, but if you need to dress up the look, adding a tailored jacket and high heels is an easy way to do it.

SWEATERS
AND
JACKETS

CABLE-KNIT SWEATER

It's one of those trusty winter items that you probably don't give much thought to when you're getting dressed on a frosty morning, but the cable-knit sweater could probably tell some pretty good stories, if it could talk. In fact, some argue that the sweater doesn't even need to be able to talk in order to tell its stories: originally worn by fishermen and farmers, the shapes that you'll find on the front are more than just pretty patterns, and were originally used to denote the wearer's clan and profession. So, a diamond-knit pattern might denote a farmer's fields, a classic cable could represent the rope used on a fishing boat, and so on.

While it's a little sad to acknowledge that today's cable knits aren't nearly as personalized as their predecessors were (or as waterproof, for that matter!), the good news is that they've come a long way from their fishing and farming roots, meaning that there are now many more ways to style them, too.

SEE ALSO

Leather Jacket, p. 104
Knee-High Boots, p. 142

HOW TO WEAR IT

1   2   3   4   5

1. PENCIL SKIRT AND HEELS

Almost anything can be dressed up with a tailored skirt and a pair of high heels—cable-knits included. A tighter fit will look more streamlined.

2. JEANS AND LEATHER JACKET

The casual uniform of choice for many, jeans and a leather jacket can be teamed up with a chunky cable-knit for extra warmth.

3. A-LINE SKIRT
A cable-knit sweater probably isn't something that you associate with eveningwear, but it can create a cute look for the holiday season when worn with a dressy skirt and heels.

4. SKINNIES AND SHIRT
Pair a neutral cable-knit with jeans and a plaid shirt for a country look.

5. JEANS AND BOOTS
For those winter days when you just want to get out the door fast, but still look like you've made an effort, try wearing a cable-knit sweater with jeans and tall leather boots.

TURTLENECK SWEATER

Despite the rather unglamorous sounding name, turtleneck sweaters can be a surprisingly chic option for cold weather dressing, as anyone who's seen Audrey Hepburn wear one in *Funny Face* will surely testify.

The tight black turtleneck, once the uniform of beatniks and artists (ideally struggling ones, living in Parisienne garrets), is far from the only option, and although the turtleneck gets a bad rap from those who associate them with dowdy dressing, the high-neck style can also be the ultimate in comfort dressing, and the sartorial equivalent of pulling on a giant hug. If you think that you can't wear a turtleneck because you're too big in the bust or not the right shape, put down that glossy magazine with its list of "rules" and then remember that it's only knitwear, and there are so many varieties of turtleneck available that you'll surely be able to find one that works just for you.

SEE ALSO

Miniskirt, p. 44
Pleated Skirt, p. 48

1   2   3   4   5

1. SHAWL, CLUTCH, AND HEELS

Brighten up a monochrome outfit with a brightly colored shawl, made suitable for eveningwear when teamed with clutch and heels.

2. SWEATPANTS AND SNEAKERS

Go sports-luxe by wearing a cashmere turtleneck with high-quality jogging pants and a pair of iconic sneakers.

3. SKINNY JEANS A slouchy turtleneck

can look good with tight jeans: leave it untucked to keep the look casual, and tie an overshirt around the waist for added laidback style.

4. PLEATED SKIRT A pleated or flowy

skirt needs something fitted on top to give the look some shape: a thin-knit turtleneck is a good option for cooler days.

5. MINISKIRT AND BOOTS

The higher the hem, the higher the neckline—a miniskirt and tucked-in turtleneck are the perfect partnership, especially if you're into the beatnik, or 60s-inspired, look.

CASHMERE CREWNECK

Cashmere has long been associated with luxury, and was even considered something of a status symbol in the past. Nowadays, the comparatively lower price of cashmere, coupled with the fact that it's more readily available, has made it more accessible, compounding its status as a closet staple. If pure cashmere is still too costly, you can pick up a cashmere blend, which will have a similar look and feel, but a lower price tag.

The crewneck sweater is a classic item, no matter what it's made from. Cashmere is particularly popular because as well as being soft against the skin, the natural fiber has the ability to keep you cool in summer and warm in winter. The rounded neckline of the crewneck makes it ideal for layering, with a shirt or T-shirt underneath, while the wide variety of colors and patterns available ensures its versatility. This kind of sweater is so useful that you might find yourself wanting one in every color!

SEE ALSO

Full Skirt, p. 40
Capri Pants, p. 124

HOW TO WEAR IT

1   2   3   4   5

1. JEANS AND SCARF A printed scarf adds both interest and warmth to an otherwise plain outfit.

2. BUTTON-DOWN SHIRT Layer your sweater over a plain shirt to create a professional look; choose a bright color to give it a bit of character.

3. SUMMER SKIRT Tuck a fitted crewneck sweater into a flowy skirt to create a bohemian-inspired look, which is brought up-to-date by keeping shoes and accessories simple.

4. PENCIL SKIRT A plain pencil skirt and fitted cashmere crewneck is the ultimate in work-appropriate chic.

5. CAPRI PANTS AND HEELS A perfect smart/casual combination for the evening, cropped pants and heels work well with a cashmere sweater. Add statement jewelry if you want to dress it up even further.

HEAVY WOOL CARDIGAN

What do you get when you cross a cardigan with a coat? It sounds like the start of a bad joke, but the answer to this question—a "coatigan"—is a useful item of clothing, which comes into its own during the cooler months of the year.

Particularly useful during the transitional months (often the trickiest to dress for), when it's too warm for a coat but not quite warm enough to go without one, this kind of cardigan is a practical layering piece. Less bulky than a wool coat, the heavy wool cardigan is a more comfortable option for wearing around the house or for travel. As cardigans in this style tend to be hip-length or longer, they also work well with things like leggings or tight jeans, and because they're so versatile, you can wear them over pretty much anything, just as you would any other item of outerwear.

SEE ALSO

Tailored Black Pants, p. 118
Clutch Bag, p. 152

1 2 3 4 5

1. TAILORED PANTS Metallic accessories and a pair of tailored pants will help to smarten up the look of a slouchy cardigan, while keeping the style loose and relaxed.

2. JEANS AND ANKLE BOOTS Layer a thick wool cardigan over a tank top and jeans, and add a pair of ankle boots for weekend-wear simplicity at its best.

3. BRETON AND JEANS The modern uniform of longline cardigan, Breton top, and skinnies is one that will take you almost anywhere. Wear it with flat knee-high boots for unbeatable smart/casual style.

4. CLUTCH AND HEELS Swap your boots for heels, and your shoulder bag for a clutch, and you have a more polished version of a classic look.

5. SHORTS Even in summertime, a cardigan can be handy: you never know when the weather is going to turn chilly!

SWEATSHIRT

Once the uniform of gym bunnies and slobs alike (strange, but true), the sweatshirt is going through an unexpected surge in popularity. Why? One word: slogans. You can probably blame this on social media, because first came the inspirational quotes, and then the inspirational clothes—or the slogan sweatshirt, as you might know it.

Popular though this look is, not all sweatshirts have slogans, and not all slogans are inspirational either: in fact, you'll find sweaters with everything from random French phrases to the names of sports teams and cities. Speaking of sports, that's where this look started, with gray sweatshirts bearing a team's name, and designed for comfort and practicality, rather than style. Sweatshirts are still comfortable and practical, obviously, but as for style? Well, that's up to you to add.

SEE ALSO

Capri Pants, p. 124
Boyfriend Jeans, p. 128

1 2 3 4 5

1. BOYFRIEND JEANS AND BOOTS

Boyfriend jeans always look good with slogan sweatshirts. If the look is a little too casual for your tastes, just add a nice pair of boots for a more dressed-up vibe.

2. PENCIL SKIRT

For a smart casual look, that's perfect for the office, try teaming a slogan sweatshirt with a pencil skirt.

3. CAPRI PANTS

Pair bright capri pants with a sweater for a relaxed but classic look that can be worn anywhere.

4. FULL SKIRT AND HEELS

Dress up a sweatshirt with a full skirt and a pair of pointed heels, to create a contemporary, fashion-forward look.

5. BLACK PANTS AND BALLET FLATS

Surprisingly chic, team either a plain or slogan sweatshirt with black pants and ballet flats.

CROPPED CARDIGAN

The 7th Earl of Cardigan probably isn't the first person who springs to mind when you're thinking about fashion icons, let's be honest. Coco Chanel, on the other hand, might just make the cut, and while it was the 7th Earl who gave the cardigan its name (it was originally a woolen waistcoat, worn by British soldiers during the Crimean War), it was Chanel who made it fashionable. Why? Well, because she didn't like the way that sweaters messed up her hair when she pulled them on!

Its ease of use, of course, is the main reason that the cardigan remains popular. It provides the perfect accompaniment to all of those sleeveless tops and dresses that it's often too chilly to wear. Cropped versions can be particularly flattering, as they don't hide too much of your figure or the outfit that you're wearing.

SEE ALSO

Dressy Top, p. 78
Tailored Black Pants, p. 118

1   2   3   4   5

1. DRESSY TOP AND PANTS

Why is the office air-con always cranked up to "Arctic?" Beat the chill by layering a cute, cropped cardigan over a dressy top and tailored pants.

2. VINTAGE-STYLE DRESS

Belt your cardigan at the waist to create an hourglass effect on almost any figure. Wear over a vintage-style dress for romantic, summer style.

3. BEACH DRESS A cropped cardigan

is a useful part of your vacation arsenal, allowing you to take a beach-appropriate dress from day to night, while fending off the evening chill.

4. SKIRT AND TIGHTS Button your

cardigan all the way up and wear it with a skirt and tights for a chic, work-appropriate look.

5. EVERYDAY JEANS A brightly

colored cardigan worn with blue jeans and sneakers creates the perfect smart/casual look for every day.

SLOUCHY SWEATER

Slouchy knitwear will always be popular, simply because it's so comfortable to wear. But how on earth are you supposed to wear it, without looking like it's laundry day, and you're all out of options? The key is to choose your sweater wisely. Remember, not all slouchy sweaters are created equally, and "the bigger, the better" probably isn't the best motto here. Rather than supersizing your sweater, choose a style that's slouchy without being sloppy—it should be loose and comfortable, without drowning you in fabric or making you feel like you're wearing someone else's clothes.

Fabric is key here, and soft, fluid knits like cashmere or silk blends will work better than stiff wool or scratchy mohair.

SEE ALSO
Ankle Boots, p. 144
White Sneakers, p. 146

1   2   3   4   5

1. SILK SKIRT A slouchy sweater can be surprisingly sexy when paired with a silk skirt.

2. MIDI SKIRT AND BOOTS Wear your sweater with a midi skirt and pair with ankle boots for a casual look that's a little more interesting than jeans.

3. JEANS AND HEELS If you do want to wear jeans with an oversized sweater, make sure that they're skinny, and add a pair of high heels to polish the look.

4. SKIRT AND SATCHEL A slim-cut skirt and structured satchel add a touch of elegance to a soft sweater.

5. PANTS AND SNEAKERS For a weekend spent shopping or relaxing, a slouchy sweater works perfectly with comfortable pants and a pair of sneakers.

BLACK BLAZER

The classic blazer might seem a little dull to some, but try telling that to the members of the Lady Margaret Boat Club, whose blazing-red jackets helped to coin the term back in the nineteenth century. In fact, try telling it to anyone with a beautifully tailored black blazer tucked away in their closet, because every blazer-lover knows that this one item is the magic ingredient that pulls your closet together, and makes it look like you've made an effort, even when you haven't. It's your closet's secret weapon, in other words.

The right blazer has the ability to add instant polish to almost any outfit, and it will never go out of style. Well, how many other nineteenth-century trends still look current? Exactly.

SEE ALSO

Pencil Skirt, p. 46
Skinny Jeans, p. 120

1   2   3   4   5

1. JEANS AND SNEAKERS It doesn't get much more laidback than jeans and sneakers, but a structured blazer will prevent the outfit from looking too casual.

2. ROMPER AND HEELS A romper and heels are a youthful alternative to a dress for evenings out or vacations. A blazer helps add sophistication to the look; replacing heels with flats would make it a touch more casual.

3. PENCIL SKIRT Despite their nautical origins, most people tend to associate blazers with the office—and with good reason, too. A well-cut blazer, paired with a pencil skirt, is the office uniform that always works. Soften the silhouette with a silky camisole or blouse.

4. LEGGINGS AND TOP If looking office-appropriate is the last thing on your mind, a blazer will give a touch of sophistication to leggings and a dressy top.

5. TAILORED PANTS Swap your pencil skirt for a pair of tailored pants to make your blazer work overtime in the office.

DENIM JACKET

Without the denim jacket, we wouldn't have something to throw over our shoulders on a cool summer evening, or an easy way to tone down the dressiness of a little black dress. On the other hand, we wouldn't have any number of 1980s fashion crimes, or those photos of Britney and Justin wearing matching double denim, which makes the denim jacket something of a double-edged sword, in style terms. There are those who'll defend it to the death and wouldn't consider their closet complete without one, and then there are those who just can't get those 80s popstars out of their head, no matter how hard they try.

What those who love their denim jackets know, however, is that blue denim is one of the few colors out there that works with just about anything, and as this style of jacket has the ability to make almost any outfit look casual, it's the perfect partner for the perpetually overdressed.

SEE ALSO

Summer Dress, p. 52
Ankle Boots, p. 144

1   2   3   4   5

1. SPORTY HOODIE It's one of the most casual pieces of outerwear around, so it makes sense that the denim jacket would look good with equally casual pieces, such as a hoodie and leggings.

2. ANKLE BOOTS AND MINISKIRT Take your denim jacket from daytime into evening with ankle boots and a miniskirt.

3. RELAXED PANTS Day off? Throw a faded denim jacket over loose pants and a sweater for easy, effortless style, topped off with a well-placed boho scarf.

4. SUMMER DRESS A lightweight denim jacket works well over a sundress, and will help warm you up on a cooler than anticipated summer's day. Team with a straw hat and a tote for the ultimate traveler chic.

5. STRIPED PENCIL SKIRT Classic blue denim is one of the most versatile shades around, and it works particularly well with nautical-inspired stripes, for a look that could even work for the office.

LEATHER JACKET

Worn by everyone from pilots to punks, the leather jacket has truly earned its place in the fashion hall of fame. It somehow manages to be edgy yet classic, warm but not hot, casual yet dressy, all at the same time—which is why it's never gone out of fashion, despite having been around for longer than most of the people who wear one.

It's probably not going to go out of style anytime soon, either. Leather jackets come in many shapes and forms, and they come in a wide variety of colors, too, with pastels and brights becoming almost as popular as the more traditional black and brown. They're one of those items that only seem to improve with age, so see it as an investment purchase and take heart from the fact that you'll probably own it forever, and will never run out of different ways to style it.

SEE ALSO

Denim Shirt, p. 70
White T-shirt, p. 74

HOW TO WEAR IT

1   2   3   4   5

1. CULOTTES AND HEELS For an informal take on office wear, a biker jacket gives a contemporary edge to culottes and heels.

2. SCARF AND KNIT DRESS Layer up your leather with a chunky scarf and wear over a knit dress and tights, to warm up on winter days.

3. JEANS AND DENIM SHIRT A leather jacket helps to break up the double-denim look, and provides a new spin on the biker jacket and jeans look.

4. JEANS AND TEE It's a look most associated with stars like James Dean and Marlon Brando, sure, but the good ol' leather jacket, blue jeans, and T-shirt combination will work just as well on almost anyone.

5. PLEATED SKIRT A structured biker jacket balances out a floaty pleated skirt, keeps the look contemporary, and adds a masculine edge to an otherwise feminine outfit.

CAMEL COAT

If you're thinking that camel is just a color, and that camel coats have nothing to do with actual camels, well, you're in for a bit of a surprise, because the name of the color we know as camel comes from the name of the animal, the hair of which was originally used to make coats, among other things.

While some higher-end camel coats are still made from camel hair, most of the versions that you'll find in the more affordable price ranges are wool (or wool blends), which are simply camel-colored. And it's the color that is mostly responsible for the popularity of this style of coat: it really does work well with everything, which is why you'll often find the word "classic" used to describe it. While you'll find camel coats in different shapes, the classic style is generally longer-line, and either belted, double-breasted, or with a single-button fastening to create a simple, unfussy shape.

SEE ALSO

Pleated Skirt, p. 48
White Sneakers, p. 146

1   2   3   4   5

1. BLACK SWEATER AND SKINNIES

Like camel itself, black never goes out of fashion, and a well-fitting, all-black outfit under a camel-colored coat will always look elegant.

2. PLEATED SKIRT
The versatility of the camel coat means that you can wear it over just about anything. With skirts, keep hems the same length as the coat (or shorter), for a streamlined look.

3. MINISKIRT AND TIGHTS

Certainly a look that's smart enough for the office, a miniskirt and tights will give a polished daytime look.

4. SKINNIES AND SNEAKERS

Wear tight blue jeans with your coat for a look that's casual without being sloppy. White sneakers provide an attractive contrast with the camel color.

5. BLACK PANTS, BRETON, AND FLATS
For the ultimate in classic style, try wearing your camel coat with other wardrobe essentials, like a Breton top, black pants, and ballet flats.

PEACOAT

Who would've thought we'd end up owing so much of our modern closets to the naval officers of the last century? As well as Bretons and blazers (see pages 76 and 100), they also brought us the peacoat. You'll be relieved to know that the peacoat has absolutely nothing to do with peas, but comes from the Dutch word "pijjekker," the first letters of which refer to the durable twill fabric used on the Dutch navy's short double-breasted coats.

Those original peacoats were dark blue in color, but you'll also find this style in camel, black, or a range of brighter shades. Stylistically, the look created by the coat is smart and preppy, and although these coats are worn casually, they tend to look a little more polished than some other types of outerwear.

SEE ALSO
Miniskirt, p. 44
Ballet Flats, p. 136

1   2   3   4   5

1. FLATS AND TOTE Although peacoats are most often associated with fall and winter, you can easily pair them with coordinating tote and flats for a fresh spring look too.

2. BRETON TOP The peacoat's naval background makes Breton stripes an obvious pairing, but one that really works.

3. MINISKIRT AND BOOTIES When wearing coats with skirts, make sure that the hem of the skirt doesn't peek out from beneath the coat, or it can look a little untidy. That rule can be tricky to observe with peacoats, but on the other hand, it does make them perfect for miniskirts and a night out in the city.

4. SLIM PANTS AND SWEATER A classic wool coat is an essential part of any professional wardrobe, and looks effortless with slim pants and a cashmere sweater.

5. SCARF AND BOOTS A chunky-knit scarf worn with knee-high boots and a classic peacoat makes for an easy winter uniform.

TRENCH COAT

No one who's seen Audrey Hepburn crying in the rain at the end of *Breakfast at Tiffany's* could doubt the style credentials of the classic Burberry trench coat that she's wearing. The original wearers of the trench had a different set of credentials, because while the style wasn't developed specifically for soldiers, it was in the trenches of World War I that the garment got its name. Burberry supplied over half a million coats to the British Army during the war, and the style continued to be worn afterward, although this time by civilians.

Traditionally, the trench coat is beige, khaki, or camel, and comes in a waterproof fabric with a double-breasted cut, a storm-flap at the back, and straps around the wrists. Most of these details hark back to the garment's military heritage, and are designed to make it as water-resistant as possible. Modern versions come in a variety of styles and colors.

SEE ALSO

Little Black Dress, p. 56
Skinny Jeans, p. 120

1   2   3   4   5

1. COCKTAIL DRESS The classic feel of a trench coat means that it can be worn over eveningwear. Try draping it over your shoulders to make it a little more glam.

2. JOGGERS AND HOODIE Throw your trench over a relaxed pair of joggers and a hooded sweatshirt for a look that's as contemporary as it is comfortable.

3. SCARF If trench coats have one fault, it's that they're too lightweight for the coldest temperatures. Try wearing a cozy scarf to warm yours up.

4. MIDI DRESS Trench coats come in various different lengths, with the shortest versions working well with miniskirts and midi or short dresses.

5. SKINNY JEANS AND HEELS One of the most classic ways to wear a trench coat is with skinny jeans and heels: a look that's smart enough for a casual office and sophisticated enough for drinks afterward.

PARKA

Puffy, occasionally fluffy (thanks to the fur-trimmed hood), and sometimes incorrectly described as an "anorak," the parka probably isn't something that you'd usually associate with glamour—or even style, for that matter. In fact, it's more like a giant duvet.

Glamorous it may not be, but let's face it: no one can be glamorous all the time, and when practicality takes over, the parka comes into its own. It's the outerwear you reach for on the coldest winter days or when you're taking part in outdoor activities; and if you've been paying attention to your favorite Pinterest boards, you've probably noticed that its use doesn't have to be limited to the purely practical. No, the humble parka is unlikely to win any style awards, but that doesn't mean that it can't look stylish anyway—you just have to know how to wear it!

SEE ALSO
Ballet Flats, p. 136
Ankle Boots, p. 144

1   2   3   4   5

1. ANKLE BOOTS AND JEANS

For casual winter days, a cozy parka will work well with ankle boots and jeans.

2. CHUNKY BOOTS AND JEANS

Toughen up your look with a bit of biker chic—ripped black jeans paired with chunky boots.

3. SKINNIES AND HEELS
Not only will a parka give your evening look of heels and cropped skinnies a contemporary edge, it'll also keep you warm on the walk home.

4. BALLET FLATS AND BLACK PANTS
Ballet flats and black ankle-length pants have the ability to make almost anything look effortlessly stylish, perfect for weekend outings.

5. WIDE-LEG PANTS AND SANDALS
Heeled sandals will give your wide-leg pants a flattering, longer look, while adding chic to an otherwise casual ensemble.

JEANS
AND
PANTS

CHINOS

"Smart/casual"—it's the dress code that everyone dreads, because it's just so difficult to interpret. Given that most of us don't own too many clothes that would pass as both smart and casual, we go into these events knowing that we're bound to be either underdressed or overdressed. So, what's a girl to do? Well, first of all, you can stop panicking, because in the battle between underdressed and overdressed, overdressing should always win.

There is, however, another reason not to panic when faced with a smart/casual dress code, and that reason can be found in a pair of chinos. The classic chino is the perfect solution to the smart/causal problem. These hardwearing twill trousers have saved many a day—sartorially speaking—and they can save yours, too. All you have to do is own a pair, and know how to style them.

SEE ALSO

Dressy Top, p. 78
Slouchy Sweater, p. 98

1   2   3   4   5

1. TAILORED JACKET AND HEELS

Add a tailored jacket, cropped cardigan, and heels to a classic pair of chinos, and you've got the smart/casual look nailed for the office.

2. SANDALS AND BOLERO A tucked-in
top underneath a bolero is a streamlined vacation look that's perfectly completed with sandals.

3. SILK TOP They're not normally
thought of as eveningwear, but a silk top and leather shoes will give a high-quality look to even an inexpensive pair of chinos.

4. T-SHIRT AND SNEAKERS

If the invitation just says "casual," sneakers and a T-shirt are the no-thought outfit that, when paired with a pair of chinos, will actually look like you *did* put some thought into it. Don't worry, your secret's safe here ...

5. SLOUCHY SWEATER AND
FLATS Roll up the hems of your chinos
and wear them with a slouchy sweater and flats for a stylish but relaxed weekend look.

TAILORED
BLACK PANTS

Black pants are to the working wardrobe
what blue jeans are to the casual one:
they're one of those items that you reach
for on days when you just don't know
what else to wear. Even if you don't work
in an office, tailored pants are a handy
item to have in your closet: not only are
they easy to style, they're also suitable for
most occasions, which is why they make
such a great fallback piece.

If you have a pair of black tailored pants,
then you *do* always have something to
wear—you just have to figure out how
to do it. The key is to make sure that
you have the right pair of black pants.
As these are an item that you're likely
to wear over and over again, it's a good
idea to invest in the best quality that you
can afford and, as with everything in your
closet, the perfect fit is essential.

SEE ALSO
Turtleneck Sweater, p. 88
White Sneakers, p. 146

1   2   3   4   5

1. HEELS AND LACE TOP Elevate your daywear by swapping jeans for cigarette pants, and cotton T-shirts for lace or embroidered versions. The look is still casual, but a little more special.

2. DRESSY TOP Evenings out don't have to mean tight dresses or skirts: a structured top and a pair of tailored cigarette pants can make a stylish alternative to the little black dress.

3. SNEAKERS AND T-SHIRT Although pants are often thought of as a dressier option than jeans or leggings, they can still work well with sneakers and a T-shirt, for a casual look with a touch of polish.

4. TURTLENECK AND FLATS For work, a fine-knit turtleneck worn with ankle-length pants and flats will create a smart/casual look with a hint of Hepburn.

5. SUMMER TOP AND FLATS Pair loose-fitting ankle pants with a linen top and casual loafers for an easy vacation look that will keep you cool and comfortable in the sun.

SKINNY JEANS

Skinny jeans have been popular for such a long time now that it's hard to remember when they weren't in fashion. Denim styles change with the decades, though: the 70s had flares, the 80s had acid wash, the 90s had high-waisted "mom" jeans, and the 2000s were the era of the bootcut. Now, skinnies are back in fashion, but it is "jeans" in the broad sense of the word that are the wardrobe essential, rather than one specific cut, because you never know when that skinny leg might start to look as dated as flares do now!

On the subject of skinny legs, one of the biggest misconceptions about skinny jeans is that you have to be equally skinny to wear them. Happily, this just isn't true. Jeans are definitely one of the harder items to shop for, but if you find the right fit, skinny jeans can work for everyone, so don't let the name put you off.

SEE ALSO

Silk Blouse, p. 80
White Sneakers, p. 146

1   2   3   4   5

1. BLAZER AND SHIRT If your workplace allows denim, try wearing skinny jeans with a blazer and shirt for a modern, but still professional, look.

2. SNEAKERS No weekend wardrobe would be complete without some combination of jeans and sneakers—it's the ultimate in casual dressing.

3. SILK BLOUSE If standard blue jeans feel too casual, glam it up with a pair of dark-wash or black skinnies and a silk blouse, for a sophisticated, off-duty look.

4. SILK SHIRT AND LEATHER JACKET Dark-wash or black jeans are classic enough to work with a silk shirt and leather jacket for smart/casual events.

5. SUMMER TOP, HAT, AND SANDALS Skinny jeans can still work in summer—just add a floaty top, sun hat, and sandals.

BLACK LEGGINGS

It might have taken you a while to get on board with the idea of leggings being more than just loungewear. But every legging-wearer knows that this much-maligned item of clothing is one of the most comfortable things that you'll ever wear, and that alone is reason enough to want to buy a pair.

You can also take comfort in the fact that today's leggings are generally pretty high quality. They tend to be thicker and stretchier and, while cheaper leggings will still be prone to the dreaded sagginess around the knees, a good quality pair will stay in place all day, and won't turn transparent after a couple of washes.

When styling leggings, bear in mind that although they might look like skinny jeans, leggings are not pants, and shouldn't be worn as such. Make sure that your top is crotch-length or longer, and you're good to go.

SEE ALSO

Sweatshirt, p. 94
Knee-High Boots, p. 142

1   2   3   4   5

1. LOOSE TOP Leggings travel well, and take up virtually no space in your luggage. Wear them with a loose-fitting top for a relaxed, on-vacation style.

2. FITTED TOP AND HEELS
Although it breaks the "top below crotch" rule (see opposite), for those who love the streamlined bodycon look, a fitted top and heels can turn basic black leggings into clubwear essentials.

3. SWEATSHIRT AND BEANIE
Layer a cozy sweatshirt over your workout look, and add a cute wooly hat on colder days.

4. LONGLINE TANK Sportswear doesn't have to be reserved for the gym: a longline tank over leggings is a laidback, casual look that you can wear all day.

5. SHIRT AND BOOTS A longline shirt and knee-high boots will cover up most of your leggings, and make for a cute, casual weekend look.

CAPRI PANTS

One item of clothing, many different names. You might know them as pedal pushers, clam diggers, cropped pants, or any one of a number of different terms. The item being described, however, is exactly the same—a pair of pants which are longer than shorts, shorter than regular pants, and normally made from a lightweight fabric. Capri pants are named after the island of Capri, and Grace Kelly was one of their early adopters. The style is associated with many of the other female stars of that era (the 50s and 60s), and has a retro glamour that is understated and easy to wear.

The length of capri pants can vary from just above the ankle to just below the knee. They are most often worn in spring and summer, and almost always as part of a casual ensemble, whatever the style or color, although it's always possible to dress them up a little.

SEE ALSO

Dressy Top, p. 78
Denim Jacket, p. 102

1   2   3   4   5

1. LIGHTWEIGHT JACKET AND SANDALS Capri pants are a summer essential, and are given a fresh look when worn with a light jacket and sandals.

2. DRESSY TOP Rock the Sandy from *Grease* look in a pair of tight capri pants worn with an off-the shoulder top, and a whole lot of attitude.

3. KNOTTED SHIRT AND PEEP-TOES Wear your capri pants with a knotted shirt and high-heeled peep-toe shoes for 50s-inspired style. Cat-eye flicked eyeliner completes the look.

4. BLAZER AND BRETON A fail-safe style formula, the blazer and Breton works just as well with capri pants as it does with any other item of clothing—where would we be without it?

5. DENIM JACKET AND TEE An easy, preppy option for a pair of brightly-colored capris is a denim jacket and white T-shirt.

WHITE JEANS

Blue jeans will always be considered a classic, but when warmer weather rolls around, a pair of white jeans can offer a more summery alternative. White jeans allow you to create the same basic looks as your faithful old blue denim, but the lighter, brighter color will give all of those looks a new lease of life, and allow you to give your casual wardrobe a seasonally-appropriate facelift.

White jeans are not without their issues, however, and can be far less forgiving than darker shades of denim. As white jeans often come in lighter-weight cotton, suitable for warmer temperatures, they have a tendency to be slightly clingy, or even transparent—not a good look. As always, the answer here is to shop around, find the right fit, and be prepared to invest more in the right pair. Cheaper is not better when it comes to light-colored denim!

SEE ALSO
Slouchy Sweater, p. 98
Peacoat, p. 108

HOW TO WEAR IT

1   2   3   4   5

1. BRETON AND PEACOAT Normally seen as a "summer only" item, white jeans can work all year round. Look out for a heavyweight denim, ignore dated fashion rules about wearing white after Labor day, and pair with a classic wool coat for a luxe winter look.

2. HALTER TOP AND SANDALS
A halter-neck top and sandals create a simple, easy-to-wear summer outfit when worn with white jeans.

3. PLAID SHIRT Just like their blue-denim sisters, white jeans work perfectly with a classic plaid shirt, for an understated but still stylish look.

4. WHITE OR CREAM SWEATER
White-on-white can seem a little daunting, especially if you're prone to spillages. Try an off-white or cream sweater instead— and steer clear of red wine and ketchup!

5. SPORTY JACKET A staple of the preppy look, a varsity jacket with a pair of white jeans will always look fresh and sporty.

BOYFRIEND JEANS

Picture it: It's a lazy Sunday morning, you've just woken up at your boyfriend's place, and you don't have any clean clothes handy, so you pull on a pair of his jeans, and look as cute as a button in them all day long. Well, that's the theory, anyway. The reality for many women is that boyfriend jeans, which are loose-fitting and intentionally oversized, can be tricky to style and, if you're not careful, can make you look like you're wearing someone else's clothes.

The trick with boyfriend jeans, then, is to make sure that they're not too oversized. Some women prefer to simply go up a size in their regular jeans, to get the "boyfriend" effect without too much sagginess, while others go for the "girlfriend" jean instead, which is a slightly more fitted version.

SEE ALSO

Silk Blouse, p. 80
Nude Shoes, p. 138

HOW TO WEAR IT

1 2 3 4 5

1. JACKET AND HEELS The key to styling boyfriend jeans is to make the look seem intentional, as opposed to accidental. One way to do that is by keeping the rest of the look smart—so a tailored jacket and pair of heels will offset the casual effect of the jeans nicely.

2. HEELS AND DRESSY TOP
A simple pair of heels and a structured peplum top give even distressed jeans a glam feel for a night out.

3. SILK BLOUSE Shirts and blouses look best when they're tucked into boyfriend jeans, rather than left loose. Try a silk blouse in a fun print for after-work drinks.

4. SLOUCHY SWEATER
Loose-fitting jeans and a slouchy sweater are the ultimate in casual, weekend essentials, which are so comfortable you won't want to take them off.

5. CASUAL COAT Step-hem jeans and a casual coat make for a very on-trend look, perfect for those who love sporty style.

WIDE-LEG PANTS

Although the fashion world has favored the skinny leg for a long time now, for those of you who don't feel like wrangling your legs into a pair of drainpipe jeans every morning, the good news is that they're far from the only option available. Wide-leg pants have been around since the 1920s, and they come in many different forms: from the flares of the 70s, through to the boot-cut styles of the 2000s, to the palazzo pants that many of us have thrown into our suitcases for a holiday in the sun.

If you don't want a full-length version, culottes are a surprisingly stylish cross between pants and a skirt, combining the look of the latter with the practicality of the former. Worn with heels for work, and sneakers afterward, they're just as versatile as those skinny jeans—and maybe a little more comfortable!

SEE ALSO

Silk Cami, p. 72
Flat Sandals, p. 134

1   2   3   4   5

1. SNEAKERS AND CARDIGAN
Relaxed pants, longline cardigan, and nice sneakers are the perfect recipe for an easy Saturday afternoon or Sunday morning.

2. SHIRT AND FLATS A loose-fitting shirt and a simple pair of pumps create a look that's laidback, but still polished when worn with wide-leg pants.

3. SILK BLOUSE Try pairing wide-leg pants with a loose and flowy silk blouse for a slightly more relaxed spin on an old favorite.

4. DRESSY TOP AND SANDALS
They're comfortable enough to wear on the plane, casual enough for sightseeing, and dressy enough for evenings out, making wide-leg pants a good choice for a summer vacation.

5. HEELS AND SILK CAMI A pair of stilettos and a silk camisole are all you need to dress up your favorite pants for the evening.

SHOES AND ACCESSORIES

FLAT SANDALS

When the days start getting warmer, you're going to want to reach for something cool on the feet. Flat sandals can be worn in exactly the same way that you'd wear your regular flats, but the open design allows air to circulate, keeping the foot cool and comfortable, even on a hot day.

As sandals aren't always considered office-appropriate, they tend to be worn with casual outfits, although you'll find dressier options too, with embellishments or other features that make them a good alternative to heels for those who either can't or don't want to wear them.

Flat sandals come in a wide range of styles, from gladiator sandals, which lace up the leg, to flip-flops and slides, which means that, no matter what you need them for, it shouldn't be too hard to find a pair that fits your requirements.

▶ SEE ALSO
Black Tank Top, p. 82
Wide-Leg Pants, p. 130

1   2   3   4   5

1. SUMMER DRESS A loose dress will keep you cool in the summer heat, as will sandals, which makes them a perfect pairing.

2. TAILORED SHORTS Choose tailored shorts for an element of style, and add playful details like a printed jacket.

3. JEANS AND TANK TOP It doesn't get much easier than jeans, tank top, and sandals, but simple accessories like a necklace and shoulder bag will keep the look interesting.

4. WIDE-LEG PANTS Cropped wide-leg pants can take you to the beach, and then out to lunch or dinner afterward. Wear them with quality leather sandals to stop them looking too sloppy.

5. PRINTED MAXI DRESS Flat sandals are the perfect pairing with a bold-print maxi dress, and they won't take up much room in your suitcase either.

BALLET FLATS

Heels or flats? Many women are firmly in one camp or the other. The trend for flats started when Marie Antoinette took her last walk to the guillotine in a pair of high heels—talk about going out in style! Those who didn't want to emulate the French queen were quick to adopt flats as their shoe of choice, but it was the queen of style, Audrey Hepburn, who really made them popular. Some of the most iconic images of Audrey feature capri pants and ballet flats—a style that looks just as current today as it did back then.

As the name suggests, ballet flats get their name from their similarity (in shape, if not in function), from the dancing slippers worn by ballerinas, which also have a ribbon binding around the foot and a decorative bow at the toe. Traditionally, ballet flats should have a rounded toe and a very small heel, but the name can be used loosely to refer to any flat shoe, in any color or pattern.

▶ **SEE ALSO**
Capri Pants, p. 124
Clutch Bag, p. 152

1   2   3   4   5

1. FULL SKIRT AND SUNGLASSES

Wear your flat shoes with a full skirt and cat's-eye sunglasses for a 50s-inspired look that oozes style.

2. MINISKIRT

High heels with a miniskirt can be a striking look for a night out. For a more subtle look, use a pair of classic flats to tone it down for daytime.

3. CAPRI PANTS AND SHIRT

Try cropped pants and a fitted shirt with your flats for a modern take on the look that Audrey Hepburn made famous.

4. TANK TOP AND WIDE-LEG PANTS

Sticking to a simple color palette is an easy shortcut to effortless style—black ballet flats will finish the look perfectly, and steer you through all seasons.

5. DRESS AND CLUTCH

You don't have to wear heels for an evening out: a pair of patent flats will look just as cute with your favorite dress and clutch bag.

NUDE SHOES

Although the color of so-called "nude shoes" is supposed to replicate the shade of the wearer's skin tone, it rarely does. Most of the shoes described as "nude" are a pinky-beige color, although some designers, like Christian Louboutin, have released lines containing nude hues, ranging from pale pink to dark brown. So why choose a shoe that's a non-color? Simple: Wearing shoes that match (or that at least blend in with) your skin makes the leg look longer, and can be more flattering than a darker or brighter color, which has the opposite effect.

For this reason, the phrase "nude shoe" is most often used to refer to a high-heeled pump style, which will also make legs appear longer. In addition to their magical, leg-lengthening effect, nude shoes are also popular because the color works with everything: so if you could only choose one shoe color, this would be a good one to go for.

▶ **SEE ALSO**
Cocktail Dress, p. 62
Denim Shirt, p. 70

1   2   3   4   5

1. SKINNY JEANS AND BLAZER
Rock Casual Fridays in a pair of skinny jeans worn with nude heels and a structured, soft pastel blazer.

2. JEANS AND SWEATER
High heels are never exactly "casual," and nudes are no exception, but they can still be teamed with jeans and a sweater for everyday elegance.

3. BRIGHT DRESS
The "go with anything" hue of a nude pump allows the rest of your outfit to stand out against it, so have fun mixing bold colors and prints.

4. TAILORED DRESS
Nude heels often have a patent upper, which makes them dressy enough to wear with occasionwear or an office dress.

5. DOUBLE DENIM
Once considered the ultimate crime of fashion, double denim is back in style due to the popularity of the denim shirt—and nothing works better with it than a classic, nude pump.

WEDGE HEELS

For those who find heels hard to walk in, the wedge is the perfect halfway house between stilettos and flats. These heels might look high, but thanks to the way that they evenly distribute weight over the whole foot (rather than forcing the wearer to walk on tiptoes, as stilettos do), they're easier to walk in, and can feel just as comfortable as flats. In fact, some people prefer wedges to flats, as they offer more arch support.

Wedges are often casual, with cork- and rope-soled versions being popular in spring and summer. Lightweight and easy to wear, cork and rope were originally used due to a shortage of leather and wood, which forced designer Salvatore Ferragamo to get creative when he came up with the style in the 1930s. Wedges have been around in some form or another ever since, and range in design from the towering, architectural platforms of Alexander McQueen and Giuseppe Zanotti, to lower, easier-to-wear styles that you'll find in stores every summer.

▶ SEE ALSO
Boyfriend Jeans, p. 128
Wide-Leg Pants, p. 130

1   2   3   4   5

1. STRIPE TANK AND MIDI SKIRT
The nautical look is a summer classic, and red, white, and blue separates work perfectly with a pair of cork wedges.

2. WIDE-LEG PANTS
Keep cool—and smart—at work on a hot summer's day in wide-leg pants, a breathable silk shirt, and a pair of wedges in a neutral color.

3. SUMMER DRESS
Choosing the same color for your shoes and dress is an easy way to create a sophisticated summer look with plenty of impact.

4. SHORTS AND TANK
Wedges are perfect for vacations, because they're as high on comfort as they are on style—even when they're equally high of heel. Wear them with shorts and a tank top for a casual look that can be dressed up for evening with statement jewelry.

5. DISTRESSED JEANS
Wedges work effortlessly with ripped jeans and a pretty top for a sweet, floaty, summer look.

KNEE-HIGH BOOTS

Normally made from leather, knee-high boots tend to have a low, wide heel, which makes them suitable for walking. Shades of tan, chestnut, or camel are common, as is black. A flat heel and tan/brown color will give knee-high/riding boots an outdoor feel, although the style is still fairly smart, allowing it to work with a variety of different outfit options. Higher heels are of course also available.

For some people, over-the-knee or thigh-high boots will always be something of a risqué option. If you're willing to give them a go, however, over-the-knee boots can be flattering and easy to wear. The trick is to make sure the hem of your skirt or dress covers the hem of your boots, creating the look of a knee-boot, but without the unflattering line that style creates across the leg. The effect is of a much more streamlined silhouette, which appears to elongate the leg, and which eliminates the leg gape that so often happens with knee-high boots.

▶ **SEE ALSO**
Knit Dress, p. 64
Skinny Jeans, p. 120

1   2   3   4   5

1. WINTER COAT AND SKINNY JEANS Winter dressing means layers, layers, and more layers. It also means finding a great pair of boots to wear with your coat, scarf, and other winter woolies.

2. SHIRT AND PENCIL SKIRT Replace your heels with knee-highs and add tights to carry your shirt and pencil skirt through into winter.

3. A-LINE MINI AND TEE Give a nod to the 70s by wearing tan knee-high boots with a denim button-front skirt and a vintage-style graphic tee.

4. DENIM SHORTS For a high-fashion look that's not for the faint hearted, try wearing over-the-knee boots with denim cutoffs for daring festival-ready style. Team with a tan tote for extra eye-catching appeal.

5. KNIT DRESS Teaming a longline cardigan, tights, and knit dress is the kind of casually elegant look that will take you anywhere, any day, when paired with high-quality knee-high boots.

ANKLE BOOTS

Ankle boots have been around for longer than any of us can reasonably be expected to remember, but it's only in the last five or so years that they've been seen as fashion items in their own right, rather than as a casual alternative to high-leg boots.

Part of this popularity is down to the sheer range of options available. Ankle boots can be high or low heeled, and come in various colors and shapes, from elastic-sided Chelsea boots to sleek, stiletto-heeled styles. Although boots in all styles are traditionally viewed as fall/winter staples, ankle boots are increasingly being worn all year round, and will work with dresses, skirts, jeans, and pants alike.

They can also be a useful way to make a dressy outfit look more casual, or to give a classic style an edge—just add ankle boots to a midi dress or pencil skirt for a more contemporary look.

▶ **SEE ALSO**
Miniskirt, p. 44
Leather Jacket, p. 104

1   2   3   4   5

1. RELAXED JOGGERS These casual pants might seem like an unexpected pairing with ankle boots, but thanks to the sport–luxe trend, anything goes.

2. PRETTY DRESS If a dress feels too fancy, a pair of casual boots can be an easy way to tone down the look and make it more wearable.

3. DENIM SHORTS Jeans work with almost everything, and the same can be said for their summery sisters, the denim cut-offs. This look also maximizes the wear of your ankle boots, transferring them successfully into the summer season.

4. SKINNY JEANS AND LEATHER JACKET All of the best casual outfits start with a great pair of jeans and a perfectly cut white T-shirt. Add a leather biker jacket and black ankle boots to finish off the rock-based look.

5. MINISKIRT Wear black boots with your miniskirt in winter to elongate the leg—say "hello" to the illusion of endless legs!

WHITE SNEAKERS

Sneakers may be an essential part of the modern-day uniform for many people, but they're not a modern invention. In fact, canvas-topped Keds have been around since the late nineteenth century, with Adidas launching just a few decades later.

Unsurprisingly, the name "sneaker" comes from the rubber soles, which are perfect for "sneaking" in. Should sneaking not be on your agenda for the day, however, the shoes remain a solid choice for any activity that requires sure-footedness—and quite a few activities that don't, because sneakers are the ultimate in casualwear, often worn with jeans or sweatpants.

You may consider sneakers too sloppy for anything other than the most casual of occasions: classic white leather Converse or Keds, however, can look surprising stylish.

SEE ALSO

Dressy Top, p. 78
Camel Coat, p. 106

1   2   3   4   5

1. CAMEL COAT, BLACK JEANS, WHITE TEE This classic outfit is all about coordination—stick to the black/white/camel code and you can't go wrong.

2. T-SHIRT DRESS Throw on a cotton T-shirt dress with white sneakers on a hot summer's day for preppy, sporty styling.

3. TROUSER SUIT While they'd only be suitable for the most informal of offices, white sneakers can be unexpectedly effective with a tailored trouser suit. They'll also help your feet to enjoy the daily commute in style, and comfort.

4. PENCIL SKIRT AND DRESSY TOP If heels aren't your thing, a pair of white sneakers will give a pencil skirt and dressy top a completely different feel.

5. TOTE AND SKINNY JEANS A good quality leather tote and a pair of skinny pants will help dress up your white sneakers for that indispensable smart/casual look.

STRAPPY HEELS

Effortlessly glamorous—and sometimes a work of art in its own right—the strappy heel is an obvious choice for evenings out and special occasions. As with any sandal, strappy heels can also work well for summer days, with the right choice of outfit.

These shoes generally have high, stiletto heels, and will often have some kind of embellishment, such as rhinestones or sequins. Metallics are popular, as they help to dress up what can be a very simple style, but other colors can be just as effective.

At the extreme end of the strappy sandal scale, the "barely there" sandal is exactly what it sounds like: just one thin strap over the toes and another around the ankle, to hold the shoe in place. The effect is of an almost-bare foot, which makes this kind of style perfect for those times when you want the rest of your outfit to do all the talking.

▶ **SEE ALSO**

Dressy Top, p. 78
Boyfriend Jeans, p. 128

1   2   3   4   5

1. BLACK DRESS T-bar sandals are another variation on the strappy style, and look fabulous with simple dresses.

2. FULL SKIRT Barely-there sandals allow a bright, printed skirt to be the focal point of the outfit.

3. DRESSY TOP AND JEANS Brightly colored sandals help to dress up a pair of blue jeans, worn with a dressy top.

4. CAMISOLE AND TAILORED PANTS A silk camisole and tailored cigarette pants make a nice alternative to a dress for eveningwear.

5. BOYFRIEND JEANS AND BRETON Distressed boyfriend jeans contrast nicely with dressier, high-heeled sandals, which also stop the jeans looking unshapely.

METALLIC SHOES

It used to be the case that women would effectively have two different wardrobes: one for eveningwear and another for regular clothes. The lines between the two have started to blur, and it's not unusual to see people wearing fabrics and styles more often associated with evening as part of their everyday outfits.

Metallic shoes are one of those items. Gold, silver, and bronze were once mostly seen on party shoes, and although metallics continue to be popular for occasionwear, the fact that they're so versatile, matching most other colors, makes them a natural choice to wear with other outfits, too.

Metallic shoes can come in various shapes, and although heels are probably the dressiest option, there are also plenty of embellished metallic flats or wedges around. As for color, gold and silver predominate, but rose gold is also popular, and can be a more subtle option.

▶ SEE ALSO

Full Skirt, p. 40
Sweatshirt, p. 94

1   2   3   4   5

1. OFFICE SUIT Lighten up your workwear by swapping court shoes for metallic sandals during the warmer months of the year.

2. JEANS AND SWEATSHIRT Metallics—and heels—aren't just for evening: ripped jeans and a sweatshirt make for a contemporary, casual look that's suitable for everyday wear.

3. JUMPSUIT A jumpsuit and metallic sandals create a high-fashion, on-trend look for an evening out.

4. DRESSY TOP AND SKIRT Have fun mixing textures like satin and lace with the shine of your metallic heels. Just add a full skirt for a striking silhouette.

5. PARTY DRESS Head-to-toe gold (or any other metallic), achieved with a sequined dress and metallic heels, makes for a stunning holiday season party outfit.

CLUTCH BAG

The clutch bag has made the transition from being occasionwear to something that you could carry every day, if you wanted to. Simple practicality might make that less of an option—clutch bags are generally too small to carry much more than your lipstick, keys, and phone, and as they often have decorative elements, like beading or sequins, they might look a little out of place in the office.

Oversized clutches do exist, and the sight of *Sex and the City*'s Carrie Bradshaw carrying hers morning, noon, and night inspired legions of women to do the same, releasing the clutch bag from its "evenings only" pigeonhole, and bringing it firmly into the fashion mainstream.

Whether or not you're willing to downsize your life enough to fit it into a clutch bag (even an oversized one), there's no denying that a pretty clutch can be a useful part of your style arsenal.

▶ **SEE ALSO**
Dressy Top, p. 78
Trench Coat, p. 110

1 2 3 4 5

1. SHIRT AND SHORTS If you don't want to cart around a heavy tote bag, a slouchy clutch will add a touch of polish to the vacation uniform of shirt and shorts.

2. LACE DRESS A special dress requires an equally special bag to wear with it, and the clutch is the perfect accessory for wedding outfits, or other occasionwear.

3. DRESSY TOP AND PANTS Switch up your workwear style by removing your blazer and adding a top in a fun print. A colorful clutch will work for both work and play.

4. CARDIGAN AND PANTS It might not hold all of your workday essentials, but for important presentations, a clutch bag will add some sophistication to casual work clothes.

5. TRENCH COAT AND SNEAKERS At the casual end of the style scale, an oversized clutch instantly adds elegance to jeans, sneakers, and an oversized trench.

SATCHEL

If the word "satchel" reminds you somewhat uncomfortably of school days, relax—satchels have grown up and, although they have the same basic shape as a briefcase, the materials and finish will easily set them apart.

As for that shape, it has a lot in common with the cross-body bag, in that satchels generally have an extra-long shoulder strap, which allows the bag to be slung across the body. In addition, most satchels will have some kind of top handle (or two) which allows the bag to also be carried over the arm or slung over the shoulder, plus a flap at the front, which normally fastens with a metal clasp.

Modern satchels also come in a much wider range of colors than the ones you might have carried to school, which helps to prevent the bag from looking old-fashioned. Although you'll still find the usual suspects, like black and tan, lots of brands are reinventing the humble satchel in a rainbow of bright colors and soft pastel shades.

▶ **SEE ALSO**
Pleated Skirt, p. 48
Printed Dress, p. 58

1   2   3   4   5

1. BLACK PANTS, HEELS, AND BLOUSE Keep your office look suitably sophisticated by sticking to classic pieces like black pants, classic heels, and a button-up blouse.

2. SILK SHIRT AND BLACK PANTS Go straight from your desk to an evening out by switching up your shoes and accessories, going for silky fabrics and statement accessories to glam-up your black office pants.

3. SCARF AND SWEATER Bundle up for winter in cozy woolens, with a leather satchel to finish off the look. Try removing the strap and carrying your satchel like a clutch for a more elegant look.

4. PRINTED DRESS AND SANDALS The traditional styling of the satchel works well with a colorful dress and vintage-inspired sandals, and helps to keep the look fresh and modern.

5. BLOUSE AND PLEATED SKIRT For a preppy look, wear your satchel cross-body over a cap-sleeved blouse tucked into a pleated skirt.

SHOULDER BAG

The term "shoulder bag" loosely describes any style of bag with long straps, allowing it to be carried over the shoulder. Totes are one of those styles. They're generally square or rectangular, with two handles, and although some might have a fastening, most are open-topped, for easy access. So, while all totes are shoulder bags, not all shoulder bags are totes—confusing, huh?

Actually, it's not really. While shoulder bags range in style from oversized, slouchy totes to small "baguette"-style evening bags, the one thing that they all have in common is their ability to be carried over the shoulder. The most useful type of shoulder bag will be one large enough to hold all of your daily essentials, without being too heavy to carry around all day. You might also want to buy an oversized canvas tote, for vacations and trips to the beach.

▶ **SEE ALSO**
Silk Blouse, p. 80
Black Tank Top, p. 82

1   2   3   4   5

1. WHITE TANK, BLACK PANTS

Sticking to a monochrome color scheme is an easy way to create a striking outfit from the simplest of pieces, bag included.

2. SNEAKERS AND LEGGINGS The

beauty of the shoulder bag is that it will smarten up anything—even sporty sneakers, leggings, and a beanie.

3. BLACK PANTS AND SWEATER

Everyday errands will feel a lot less mundane when you carry an awesome leather shoulder bag, rather than a tatty old tote.

4. SHORTS AND BLOUSE

Tailored shorts and a silk blouse are a summery alternative to the office suit or dress, and a high-quality shoulder bag helps to keep the look professional.

5. CULOTTES The clean lines of a pair

of tailored pants or culottes work really well with a structured shoulder bag.

CROSS-BODY BAG

Cross-body bags are often smaller in size than a shoulder bag or tote, with an extra-long strap, which allows the bag to be slung diagonally from shoulder to hip.

Cross-body bags have two advantages over other styles: one is that they allow the wearer to go hands free, without having to hold onto a strap; the other is the extra security that they offer, as they're harder for passers-by to grab. For these reasons, cross-body bags can be a good choice for something like a day's sightseeing, or for when you need the use of one or both hands when out and about.

Of course, although the cross-body bag is designed to be worn as the name suggests, it can also be worn on one shoulder. Most styles have adjustable shoulder straps, which enable it to transform into a traditional shoulder bag, if required.

▶ **SEE ALSO**
Denim Jacket, p. 102
Silk Scarf, p. 162

1   2   3   4   5

1. SHIFT DRESS For those times when you're traveling extra-light (brunch or shopping, anyone?), a mini cross-body bag will carry your keys, phone, and bank card, although not much else! A contrasting colored strap will break up a single-colored shift dress.

2. JEANS, BOOTS, AND SCARF
Details like a chain strap or quilted leather fabric add interest to the bag, which can be worn effectively with jeans and boots due to its size and shape. A scarf and sunglasses complete your accessorizing.

3. MINISKIRT Adjustable straps allow your bag to be carried on one shoulder, if you prefer, making it more suitable for wearing as part of a dressy evening look.

4. DENIM JACKET AND PANTS
The security of the cross-body bag makes it a popular choice for travel—ooze city-sightseeing chic with flared pants and a denim jacket.

5. WINTER COAT As cross-body bags are generally small and unobtrusive, they're versatile enough to be worn smart or casual, for summer or winter.

LEATHER BELT

At one time, it was used to stop your trousers from falling down, but most belts now have a strictly decorative purpose. Or, at least, they should have, because if a belt is the only thing standing between you and an unfortunate "flashing" incident, then you need a new pair of trousers—and ones that fit properly—not another belt! Finding clothes that fit perfectly isn't always the easiest of tasks, but it's one of the keys to good style, so if you're relying on belts, suspenders, or other items to make sure that your outfit stays on (or up), it's probably time to go shopping.

If, on the other hand, your interest in belts comes purely from the various different styling options that they offer, then your biggest problem is probably going to be deciding how many you need, and which styles to choose. the world of belts is more varied than you might think, and the right belt will finish off your outfit perfectly.

SEE ALSO
Skinny Jeans, p. 120
White Jeans, p. 126

1   2   3   4   5

1. WHITE JEANS AND DENIM SHIRT
Tan leather looks particularly good with white or light denim, creating a fresh and classic summer color palette.

2. EVENING DRESS Use a leather belt to cinch a loose dress in at the waist, for a simple evening outfit.

3. BLACK DRESS A waist belt contrasts with a black dress, without interfering with the simple lines of the outfit.

4. CARDIGAN AND MINISKIRT
Wear a belt over a loose-fitting cardigan to define the waist and add shape. Align the belt with the top of your skirt, for extra style.

5. SKINNY JEANS AND TEE
If you want to tuck your T-shirt into your jeans, for a streamlined look, a belt is an absolute must—good quality leather is the perfect finishing touch.

SILK SCARF

Most people would be able to identify the silk scarf as one of the so-called wardrobe essentials—it's certainly cited as one often enough. Very few, however, know how to wear a silk scarf, or just how many different ways there are to do so. Of course, it can be just as simple as throwing it around your neck and heading out the door, but this particular accessory didn't become popular because there was only one way to wear it. Instead, it's the multiple different styling options—and, of course, the luxurious and beautiful fabric—that have helped the silk scarf to stand the test of time.

Scarves had been around long before the composer Beethoven started wearing them, but it was his attempt to change his image in order to impress the woman he was in love with that helped to popularize the scarf. While a change of scarf might not change your image, thanks to the various prints and styling options, at least you'll have fun trying.

▶ **SEE ALSO**
Cocktail Dress, p. 62
Trench Coat, p. 110

1   2   3   4   5

1. LONG DRESS Loop a narrow scarf once around the neck, and leave each end on different sides of the body for an elegant look when worn with a long dress.

2. HEADBAND WITH SKIRT AND HEELS Tie a colored scarf around the head and knot at the top, for 50s-inspired style. Matching scarf and heels will add unbridled glamour.

3. TRENCH AND JEANS One of the simplest ways to style a scarf is to simply tie it in a loose knot at the chest, which works well with the loose styling of trench coat and boyfriend jeans.

4. BRETON AND JEANS A silk neckerchief works well with a Breton top and jeans—just add oversized sunglasses for Parisian chic.

5. A-LINE AND BOOTS A silk scarf is another office wear staple, but looks much more contemporary when worn with an A-line skirt and knee-high boots.

SUNGLASSES

Many people mistakenly believe that sunglasses should be worn only in the summer, but they're called sunglasses for a reason—the reason being that they're designed to protect your eyes from the glare of the sun, no matter what the time of year.

That's the practical reason to wear sunglasses. They're not, however, a purely practical item, and those who love them learned long ago that sunglasses can be a powerful weapon in the war on bad style. Their magical properties include the ability to hide tired eyes, conceal a lack of makeup, and make any outfit, no matter how casual or sloppy, look that much more glamorous. These are tricks that celebrities have known forever, but you don't have to be rich and famous to use your sunglasses as an accessory, rather than a necessity, on a sunny day. All you need to know is which shape best suits your face, not to mention your personal style.

SEE ALSO

Breton Top, p. 76
Peacoat, p. 108

HOW TO WEAR IT

1   2   3   4   5

1. KAFTAN AND HEADSCARF

Head to the beach in a lightweight cover-up. A fun headscarf keeps your hair under control, while dark glasses hide mascara-free eyes.

2. HAT AND KIMONO

Wearing sunglasses with a monochrome ensemble will give you an air of mystery; a floral-print kimono lightens the look, adds style, and will stop you from looking too much like a cartoon spy.

3. WINTER COAT AND JEANS

Sunglasses aren't just for summer—the low winter sun can be even harder on the eyes than it is in summer, so make sure that you always have a pair of sunglasses stashed in your bag. They look so good, after all!

4. SUNDRESS AND SANDALS

Get all of your summer essentials into one outfit: sundress, sunglasses, and sandals will work like they were made for each other, because they pretty much were!

5. BRETON AND BOYFRIEND JEANS

The "Breton and blue jeans" formula never fails, and a pair of dark glasses gives it even more Parisian chic.

HAT

At some point in the middle of the last century, hats stopped being fashionable—to some extent, at least. They were still worn, of course, and continue to be worn, but gone are the days when you wouldn't feel fully dressed if you went out in public without a hat, and nowadays they tend to be worn only when necessary, such as for keeping your head warm in the winter or cool in summertime.

This decline in the popularity of the hat is both good news and bad news. It's good news, because restrictive dress codes can really take the fun out of fashion, and the idea that you *have* to wear something, purely to meet a societal norm, feels painfully old-fashioned to our modern sensibilities. It's bad news, because hats are pretty awesome, all things considered—and not just because they're the perfect answer to many a bad hair day. Hats can really add something to an outfit: glamour, sophistication, fun—you name it. You might not want to wear one every day, but you never know, this oft-neglected accessory could be just what your wardrobe needs.

▶ **SEE ALSO**

Pleated Skirt, p. 48
Ankle Boots, p. 144

1   2   3   4   5

1. SIXTIES' DRESS Create a fun, 60s vibe by pairing a floppy hat with a bell-sleeved mini dress and chunky jewelry.

2. MAXI DRESS Keep covered up and cool—in both senses of the word—in a cotton maxi dress, oversized hat, and equally oversized sunglasses.

3. PRINTED SHORTS Get festival-ready in printed shorts, ankle boots, and a wide-brimmed hat to keep the sun—or rain—out of your eyes.

4. HEELS AND SKIRT A floppy fedora looks effortlessly elegant with heels and a mid-length skirt.

5. PONCHO AND BOOTS Layer up for winter in a thick-knit poncho, jeans, and boots. A wool fedora adds both warmth and style.

RESOURCES

CREDITS

All location photography by Odi Caspi
All illustrations by Clare Shepherd

Models:

Danielle Court 19 (tr), 23, 29 (tr), 56, 110, 164

Emily Colclough 132 (tl), 140, 150, 166, 169

Aimy Dodge 20 (tr), 35 (tr), 39, 58, 134, 138, 156

Chandni Fokeer 16 (tr), 66 (tr), 70, 133, 152

Cherrie Ho 42, 144

Beata Kolak Mendes 142

Natalia Ortegon 20 (tl), 50, 66 (b), 72

Louise May Parker 16 (br), 29 (tl), 33, 37, 60, 67, 68, 82, 168 (tl)

Pauline Perello 12, 38, 62, 66 (tl), 78, 84 (b), 102

Alona Remez 17, 38 (tr), 46, 84 (tr), 96

Kat Ronson 38 (tl), 44, 48, 54

Kendal Smales 5 (middle right), 27, 85, 92, 112, 114 (tl), 128

Ariel Thompson 24 (br), 114 (b), 126

Additional images:

Amber McNaught 5 (far right), 16 (bl), 19 (tl), 20 (b), 24 (tr), 31, 35 (tr), 40, 80, 86, 90,94, 98, 104, 120, 124, 136, 154

Getty 5 (far right and middle left), 16 (tl), 74, 88, 106, 108, 114 (tr), 118, 130, 146, 162

Shutterstock 19 (br and bl), 35 (b), 52, 64, 76, 122, 132 (tr and b), 148, 158, 160, 168 (tr and b), 167

Stocksy 84 (tl), 100

M&Co 24 (tl and bl), 116

Clothing credits:

Armor Lux, ASOS, Atmosphere, Beauty Girls, Catisa, Clarks, Debenhams, District, Dorothy Perkins, Dune London, F&F, French Connection, GAP, George, Graceland, H&M, Hobbs, Influence, Jigsaw, John Timpson, Lilley, Kendall + Kylie, Louche, Primark, M&S, New Look, Profile, Redherring, River Island, Sandro, Star by Julien MacDonald, Sweewe Paris, Tenki, Topshop, Warehouse, Y.A.S, Zara.

RESOURCES

Hopefully this book has inspired you to find your own style, and work with the pieces shown to develop your own capsule wardrobe. However, whether you're shopping until you drop, desperately trying to track down that one item to complete the perfect outfit, or simply in need of some inspiration, browsing online can be a worthwhile undertaking.

FAVORITE STORES

Zara
www.zara.com

Good for modern classics, on-trend pieces, and some of the best shoes available in-store.

ASOS
www.asos.com

One of the Internet's biggest treasure troves of fashion, with something to suit every style, and (almost) every budget. If you can't find it here, it probably can't be found.

Boden
www.boden.com

Timeless classics, often with a retro-inspired twist, or in a fun, quirky print, Boden represents British style at its absolute best.

H&M
www.hm.com

One of the best places to find basics like T-shirts, tanks, and lingerie, plus the occasional stand-out skirt or dress—and all at a budget-friendly price, too.

Net-a-Porter
www.net-a-porter.com

Fantasy shopping at its finest: Even if your budget won't quite stretch to the designer prices, this is a wonderful source of inspiration on upcoming trends, which will soon filter down to the mall.

Modcloth
www.modcloth.com

Vintage-inspired fashion, most of which will also work in a more contemporary setting.

Shopbop
www.shopbop.com

High-quality clothing and accessories from brands like Marc Jacobs, Kate Spade, Michael Kors, and more. Plus some of the fastest shipping you'll find, even for international purchases.

Zappos
www.zappos.com

All the shoes you'll ever need, including pumps that come in too many colors to count—don't be surprised if you want to buy them all.

Kate Spade
www.katespade.com

If you love spots and stripes, you'll probably love Kate Spade, and if the clothing and accessories are a little too expensive, the brand also sells an amazing line of stationery, too.

Christian Louboutin
www.christianlouboutin.com

If you only ever buy one pair of designer shoes in your life, Christian Louboutin's "Pigalle" pumps should be that shoe: you'll want to wear them with everything!

AUTHOR'S BLOGS
www.foreveramber.co.uk

For outfit photos, beauty product reviews, and stories about my life, home, and the various things that I get up to, pop along to my blog.

www.thefashionpolice.net

An imaginary police force, dedicated to fighting crimes of fashion and helping people to find stylish solutions to their wardrobe dilemmas.

www.shoeperwoman.com

A mixture of fashion, lifestyle, and other features, all of which aim to both entertain and to help you be your own ShoeperWoman. You'll also find a lot of beautiful shoes, to either look at or buy—your choice.

INDEX

ACKNOWLEDGMENTS

This book was written during a particularly crazy and often difficult few months for me, so my thanks first of all have to go to my amazing parents and to my wonderful husband, Terry—not just for putting up with me, but for holding my hand, always being there to cheer me on, and never stopping believing in me. I couldn't have done it without you!

Thanks are also due to the readers and followers of my blog, ForeverAmber.co.uk. When I started keeping an online diary over 10 years ago, I had absolutely no idea that it would turn into a business, or lead to opportunities like this one, and it was only the endless support of my readers that encouraged me to keep on going, day after day. Without the community that built up around my blog, I would still be working in a job that I hated, and would probably have laughed at the very idea that I would one day write a book about style! So, thank you from the bottom of my heart to everyone who has commented, emailed, or otherwise simply taken a few minutes out of their day to get in touch and let me know that I haven't just been talking to myself all this time!

Finally, huge thanks to the team at Quarto for approaching me to work on this project, and for pulling it all together to create the final product. This was my first experience of working on a project of this size, and I feel very lucky to have been able to work with such talented people—thank you!